D0229398

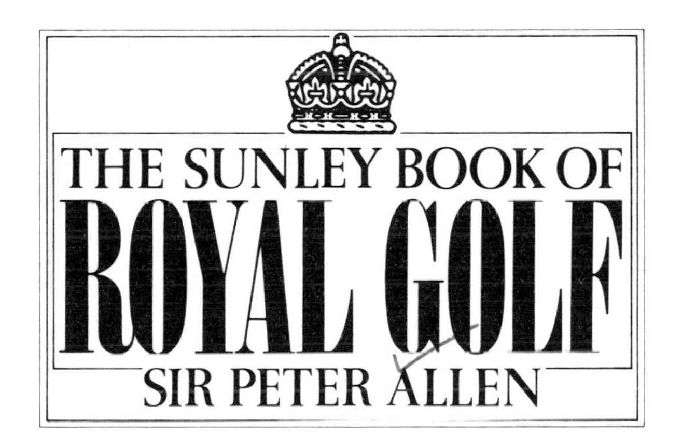
THE SUNLEY BOOK OF
ROYAL GOLF
SIR PETER ALLEN

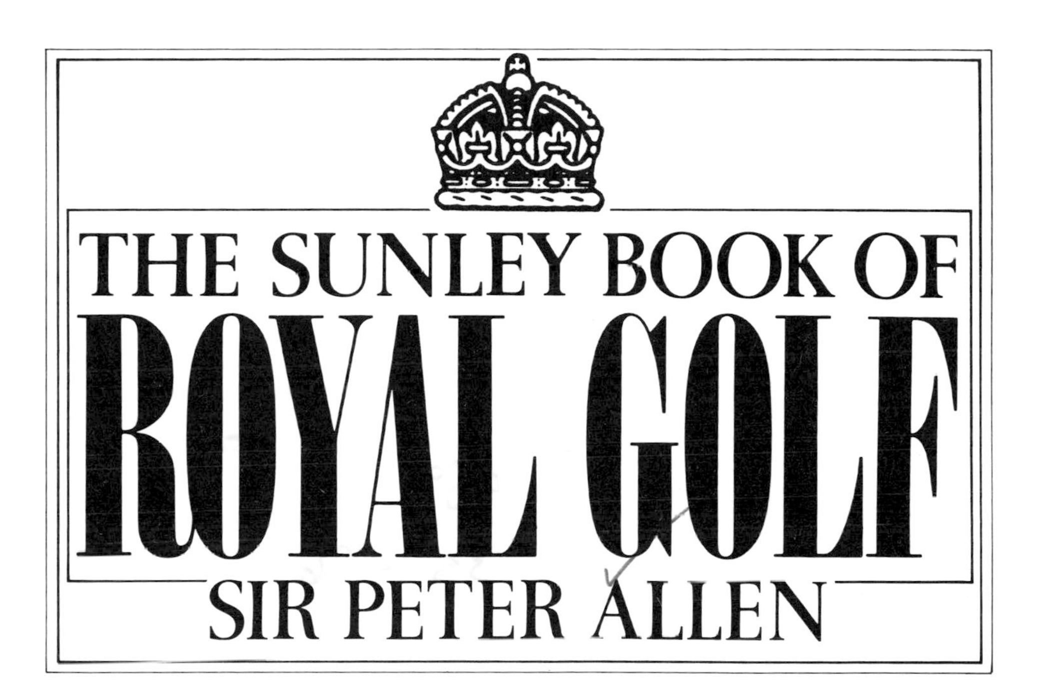

Stanley Paul
London Sydney Auckland Johannesburg

For Consuelo, who would not give up, especially in that long hard summer.

Stanley Paul & Co. Ltd

An imprint of Century Hutchinson Ltd

62–65 Chandos Place, London WC2N 4NW

Century Hutchinson Australia (Pty) Ltd
89–91 Albion Street, Surry Hills, NSW 2010

Century Hutchinson New Zealand Limited
PO Box 40–086, Glenfield, Auckland 10

Century Hutchinson South Africa (Pty) Ltd
PO Box 337, Bergvlei 2012, South Africa

First published 1989

Set in 11/12pt Times Roman

Designed by Julian Holland

Photoset by Deltatype Ltd, Ellesmere Port, Cheshire
Printed and bound in Great Britain by Butler & Tanner Ltd, Frome and London

British Library Cataloguing in Publication Data

Allen, Sir, Peter, *1905* –
The sunley book of royal golf : the story of royal golfers, royal clubs and royal courses.
1. Golf
I. Title
796.352

ISBN 0 09 173805 9

Contents

Foreword

'Royal' golf courses have always held a special place in the estimation of golfers all over the world. In my case, having been fortunate enough to have spent my early golfing days playing over the links of the Royal Cinque Ports Golf Club, Deal, and Royal St George's, Sandwich, I have been especially privileged.

Sir Peter Allen's love of the finer traditions of all sports, allied to his immense knowledge of the development of golf from its earliest days, has made this study of royal golf inevitable.

In 1963 Peter Allen became the first overseas golfer to be elected a member of the Augusta National Golf Club, personally supported by Robert Tyre Jones Jr. He was already a member of one other famous club in the United States – Pine Valley in New Jersey.

In the United Kingdom he had been, for many years, a member of the Royal and Ancient Golf Club of St Andrews, Royal St George's, the Royal Cinque Ports and also Rye.

With my long-term colleague, the late John Fryer, and my son, James, the Sunley Organization has recently completed the construction of a new golf course just outside Orlando, Florida – Lake Nona. This new club was created with a sensible ambition: to be the best. But at the same time to make a real contribution to the game – in my view a very royal and not just ancient game – that would one day, like St Andrews and Augusta, be regarded as part of our golfing heritage.

This heritage is definitively brought up to date with Sir Peter Allen's book of royal golf, with which I am very proud to be associated.

JOHN B. SUNLEY
Lake Nona
Orlando

Introduction and acknowledgements

There are more than two thousand golf clubs in the British Isles. Of these thirty-seven carry the proud title 'Royal': eighteen in England, ten in Scotland, five in Ireland, two in Wales and two in the Channel Islands.

There seemed to be many unanswered questions asked by this list, so we have tried to find out if there were some underlying reasons behind the application for and the granting of the royal title. Why, for example, are golf and yachting virtually the only sports so honoured? Why, for example, do we have the Royal and Ancient Golf Club of St Andrews, a title granted by the Monarch himself, and not the Royal Marylebone Cricket Club? And why the Royal Wimbledon Golf Club and not the Royal All-England Lawn Tennis and Croquet Club; or, in another sphere, the Royal Blackheath Golf Club but not the Royal Blackheath Rugby Football Club?

Then again the names of the golf clubs so honoured provoked questions. If fame or status came into it, why not Royal Prestwick, Royal Sunningdale or Royal Carnoustie, if less distinguished clubs are among the elect? When we look abroad at the royal clubs of the former British Commonwealth and Empire, there too are unanswered questions. Why, for example, are there eight royal clubs in Australia and none in New Zealand? How is it that there is a Royal Evian in France, and why did Royal Tara turn up in Eire after independence and Royal Sant' Anna in Italy in 1978? Why did some clubs keep their title after separation from Britain and others abandon it?

The Golfer's Handbook (that Wisden of the golf world, which usually gets things right) said: 'the right to the designation *royal* is bestowed by the favour of the Sovereign or a member of the Royal House'. While this is no doubt correct, the manner and extent of granting the honour has changed with time.

In the nineteenth century no pattern was discernible in the grant of the honour, and it seems to have been a matter of local pride and local effort to obtain it or else of some particular relationship with a member of the royal family. The grant of royal honours for golf clubs seems to have been fairly wide until 1901, when in the new reign the procedure was canalized more strictly through the Home Office or the Scottish Office – although the Prince of Wales, later Edward VII, had pointed out as early as 1882 that a royal prefix for the Wimbledon Club was a matter for which the Home Office had to give advice to the Crown. Some confusion undoubtedly arose, especially at the end of the nineteenth century, as to whether the grant of royal patronage conferred also the title 'Royal'. In some cases it was thought that it did, and in others it specifically did not. Since 1919, when procedures were reviewed again, grants of the royal title have, it is clear, been few and far between. At the conclusion of our researches we have to admit that no pattern could be found. Those that strove for the title often seem to have got it, especially in the Dominions and Empire. What has not come to light, of course, is any record of failure to attain the royal prefix.

This is not a history of golf, far from it, but inevitably some club histories are involved, and I am indebted to the clubs who have responded most handsomely to requests for information. Many, indeed most, of those concerned have sent written records which we have been allowed to draw upon.

My special thanks go to Mr Robert Burnet, the Historian of the Royal & Ancient Golf Club at St Andrews, who has taken immense trouble to look up and copy old records. His help has been invaluable. Great trouble was also taken by Mr Laurence Viney, editor of that noble work *The Golfer's Handbook*, to help me, and Mr Henry Arnell of Royal Ashdown Forest and Mr John Milton of Royal Eastbourne have gone out of their way too. We had great support from Scotland, notably from Mr Audis at Royal Burgess, Mr Baird at Royal Aberdeen, Mr Blake at Royal Perth, Mr Strachan of Royal Montrose, Mr George Hastie of Royal Musselburgh, Mr Piero at Duff House, Mr Henry at Royal Tarlair and Mr Montgomerie of Royal Troon, who provided most useful material.

All the English royal clubs contributed, especially Royal Ascot, Royal Cromer, Royal Worlington & Newmarket, Royal Cinque Ports, Royal Mid-Surrey, Royal Winchester, Royal St George's and Royal Lytham and St Annes through their Secretaries, as did Mr David Stirk of Royal Blackheath and Mr Charles Cruikshank of Royal Wimbledon.

The Secretaries of Royal Porthcawl and Royal St David's in Wales and of Royal Jersey and Royal Guernsey helped a lot, and in Ireland Royal Dublin and Royal Belfast contributed handsomely with literature. I was very grateful to Commandant Gibson of the Irish Army who took the trouble to write from the UN Peace-Keeping Force in the Lebanon about the Curragh Club in Ireland.

Mr Alan Gawler and Mr Stanley Martin were good enough to dig out some information on the defunct Royal Cornwall Club, and Mr Michael Attrill did likewise for the Royal Isle of Wight.

From abroad help flowed in, especially from the Australian clubs; notably, Mr Touzeley of Royal Melbourne, Mr Allen of Royal Sydney and Mr Cudmore of Royal Adelaide responded fully. Royal Montreal too, Royal Ottawa and the Canadian Golf Foundation, Royal Nairobi and Royal Calcutta provided literature, and Mr Annesley Keown helped with his great knowledge of Malaysia. Mr Royce Bowen made a great contribution from South Africa.

In Spain Don Luis Alvarez de Bohorquez, the Secretary General of the Spanish Royal Federation, was a valuable helper, and so were two good Spanish ladies, Mari, Sra de Milans del Bosch, and the Marquesa de San Nicolas de Noras. In Belgium Mr Roger Duys, the Secretary of the Belgian Royal Golf Federation, provided some excellent literature and opened doors at the Royal Club at Ravenstein and at Royal Antwerp.

And once again I am greatly indebted to my friend Alan Booth who has acted as Advisory Editor and also rescued me with a whole section on royal golf in Morocco.

In collecting suitable pictures the clubs have helped widely, and so have Mr Dignum of Associated Newspapers, the picture librarians of the *Illustrated London News* and of the *Radio Times* Hulton Picture Library. The loan of pictures of Malta by Richard Stafford was a kindness, and so was the loan of a wide range of transparencies by Mr Phil Sheldon. Thanks also to Hailey Sports Photographic, Peter Dateley and the Irish Tourist Board. A real prize picture was found by Mrs Gordon Goodrich of Winchelsea, and another by Major Carrington-Smith at Broncaster.

Finally my most warm and grateful thanks go to my wife Consuelo, who carried the burden when I was ill, and to Mrs Robin Harris for their kindness in carrying out so ably the drudgery of typing all this out. Miss Connie Knell, who helped with some recondite research, was also a great supporter.

In conclusion I would like to say how welcome the partnership with Sunley Holdings PLC has been in the production of this book.

ROYAL CLUBS IN THE BRITISH ISLES

		Date	Royal
1	Edinburgh Burgess	1735	1929
2	Royal & Ancient	1754	1834
3	Blackheath	1766*	1857*
4	Musselburgh	1774	1876
5	Aberdeen	1780	1903
6	Montrose	1810	1845
7	Perth	1824	1833
8	North Devon	1864	1867
9	Wimbledon	1865	1882
10	Liverpool	1869	1871
11	Dornoch	1877	1906
12	Jersey	1878	1879
13	Troon	1878	1978
14	Belfast	1881	1908
15	Curragh	1883	1910
16	Dublin	1885	1891
17	Lytham and St Annes	1886	1891
18	Ascot	1887	1887/1977
19	Eastbourne	1887	1887
20	St George's	1887	1894
21	Ashdown Forest	1888	1894
22	Cromer	1888	1888
23	Epping Forest	1888	1888
24	Portrush	1888	1893
25	Winchester	1888	1913
26	Birkdale	1889	1951
27	County Down	1889	1907
28	Guernsey	1890	1891
29	Porthcawl	1891	1909
30	West Norfolk	1891	1891
31	Cinque Ports	1892	1910/1949
32	Mid-Surrey	1892	1926
33	Norwich	1893	1893
34	Worlington	1893	1895
35	St David's	1894	1908
36	Duff House	1909	1909
37	Tarlair	1926	1926

* Or earlier

DEFUNCT	Start	Title	Died
Isle of Wight	1882	1883	1961
Eastbourne Ladies	1888	1893	1933
Cornwall	1889	1890	1939
Ashdown Ladies	1889	1932	1951
Craggan (Royal Household)	1909	1909	1939

ROYAL HOUSEHOLD

Balmoral
Windsor
Sandringham

OTHERS

Tara

CHAPTER 1

Royal Golfers

The origin of golf is uncertain, and it is not intended to go into it here. At least as early as the fifteenth century we can see a beginning of the game in Scotland, primitive as it certainly was and barely recognizable as a forerunner of, say, The Masters at Augusta. Golf may have been played at St Andrews when the University was founded in 1411. Certainly by the middle of the fifteenth century it was firmly enough established in Scotland to be interfering with the archery practice necessary to defend the realm in the wars with England.

In 1457 in the reign of James II came the well-known Parliamentary order which 'decreed and ordained the wapinschwingis be halden be the Lordis and Baronis spirituale and temporale, four times in the yeir and that the Fute-ball and Golf be utterly cryit doune and nocht usit; and that the bowe merkis be maid at ilk paroche kirk, a pair of buttis, and schutting be usit ilk Sunday'.*

* From Robert Clark, *Golf: a Royal and Ancient Game (place: pub,* 1875; repr. 1984).

King William IV (1765–1837)

King James II (1430–1460) of Scotland

Although there is no evidence that King James II played golf, this decree must have been something he was aware of. This king, known as 'James of the Fiery Face', was killed, we read in Robert Browning's invaluable *History of Golf*,† by the bursting of one of his own primitive cannon at the siege of Roxburgh Castle.

Again, thanks to *Golf: a Royal and Ancient Game* we can quote the Scottish Act of 1471, in the reign of James III, which was intended to arm the nation against 'our auld enimies of England' and which decreed that 'ilk yeman that can nocht deil with the bow, that he haf a gude ax and a targe of leddir, to resist the shot of Ingland, quhilk is na cost bot the valew of a hide . . . and that the Fute-ball and Golfe be abusit in tyme cuming and the buttis made up and schutting usit'. This too must have had royal approval, and also the order of May 1491, in the reign of James IV, which said 'That in na place of the realme there be usit Fute-ball, Golfe or other sik unprofitabill sportis, but the commoun gude of the realme, and defence thair of, and the bowis and schutting be hantit, and bowmakers maid therefore ordained in ilk parochin, under the pain of fourtie shillings, to be raised be the schireffe and baillies foresaid.'

While James II and James III may have been no more than aware of golf, James IV certainly was a player, and the Peace of Glasgow in 1502 and his marriage to the daughter of Henry VII, Princess Margaret, ended temporarily the wars with England and so allowed the game to be resumed in Scotland. James IV, it seems, was quick to take advantage of it. The accounts of the

† Robert Browning, *A History of Golf* (London: Dent, 1955).

James III (1451–1488)

James IV (1473–1513)

Lord High Treasurer of Scotland gave these reports:

1503–4	Feb 3	Item to the King to play at the Golf with The Earl of Bothuile xlij S̄
		Item to Golf Clubis and Ballis for the King that he play it with ix S̄
1505–6	Feb 22	Item for xij Golf Balls to the King iiij S̄
1506	July 18	Item the xviij of Julij for ij Golf Clubbes to the King ij S̄

Peace with England did not last long, and King James IV, 'James of the Iron Belt', died fighting on foot with his spearmen round him on the stricken field of Flodden* in 1513.

There is some evidence that at this time, in 1513, golf was at least known in England, as Catherine of Aragon, the first wife of Henry VIII, wrote to Cardinal Wolsey saying: 'And all his [the King's] subjects be very glad, Master Almoner, I thank God to be busy with the Golf, for they take it for pastime.'*

James IV's son, James V, is said to have played golf often at Godford, and his daughter, Mary Queen of Scots, who succeeded him, as has been told all too often, was criticized for playing 'golf and pall-mall in the field beside Seton' a day or so after her husband Darnley was murdered in 1567.

James VI, child of Mary Queen of Scots, who was made King of Scotland in infancy when his mother was deposed, was a keen golfer and learned the game at Perth before he came also to the throne of England in 1603. That year he appointed William Mayne 'bower [i.e. bowmaker] burges of Edinburgh, during all dayis of his lyf-time clubmaker to his Hienis'. In 1618 on a visit to his native Scotland he heard complaints that sport and recreation were prohibited on Sundays and decreed that they should be allowed after church was over, for those who had 'first done their duties to God'. This tolerance of Sunday play was confirmed by his son, King Charles I. Also in 1618, King James I granted a monopoly for twenty-one years to James Melvill for the manufacture of golf-balls, provided that he did not charge more than four shillings per ball. This monopoly was granted because too much gold and silver was going to Holland for the purchase of balls.

James VI and I's move to London, accompanied by a good number of Scots, is the foundation for the belief that a society or club of golfers was formed at Blackheath in 1608, but while golf was no doubt played there when the Court was at Greenwich there is no evidence of a *club* existing as such.

James I's elder son, Henry Prince of Wales, who died of typhoid at the age of eighteen, is reported in a Harleian manuscript in the Bodleian Library at Oxford as nearly hitting his tutor, Master Newton,

* Robert Browning, *A History of Golf* (London: Dent, 1955).

James V (1512–1542)

Mary Queen of Scots (1542–1587) supposedly playing golf at St Andrews in 1563

when playing golf, whereupon 'the Prince drawing back his hand said "Had I done so, I had but paid my debts." ' His brother, who became King Charles I, learned the game at Dunfermline and was said to enjoy it. He was playing golf at Leith in 1642 when news of the Irish Rebellion was brought to him, which it is said upset him so much that he called for his carriage and returned at once to Holyrood. Another version is that he insisted on finishing the game. Charles I is also reported as playing at Newcastle-upon-Tyne when he was held captive by the Scots in 1646.

Charles II played a little in Scotland, though after the Restoration he seems to have had other things on his mind than golf; but his brother, who briefly sat on the throne as James II, was a keen player. Robert Browning puts the well-known story of his famous match at Leith Links so well:

> By far the happiest of the Stuarts in his golfing associations was James II, who as Duke of York played frequently at Leith while resident in Edinburgh during the years 1681 and 1682 as

James VI (1566–1625)

Charles I, playing golf on Leith links in 1641, receives the news of the Irish rebellion

commissioner from the King his brother to the Scottish Parliament. As a result of a dispute between the duke and two English noblemen at the Scottish Court concerning the origin of the game, it was proposed to decide the matter by a match over Leith links in which the Englishmen would play against the duke and any Scottish partner he liked to produce. The partner recommended to the duke by the Leith worthies was a poor shoemaker named John Patersone, and it is not difficult to guess that the presence of this local artisan champion was the factor that decided this first international match. The duke and his partner were victorious and the shoemaker was dismissed with an equal share of the very considerable stake wagered on the result. With this money he built himself a house in the Canongate of Edinburgh upon the wall of which the duke caused an escutcheon to be fixed, bearing the arms of the Patersone family surmounted by a crest in the form of a dexter hand grasping a golf club, with the motto, 'Far and Sure'. The house, long known locally as 'The Golfer's Land', is still standing.* The Latin inscription, as I have seen for myself, bears out the above account as far as a Latin inscription can be expected to bear out anything, and the additional motto which the inscription bears, 'I hate no person' – an anagram on the name 'John Patersone' – also serves to confirm the traditional story.

* Alas, no more.

We have found no word of golf in the life of James II's son James, the Old Pretender, or of Mary, James II's eldest daughter, who shared the English throne with William of Orange, or of Queen Anne, James's second daughter and the last Stuart monarch.

The Old Pretender's son, Prince Charles Edward, the Young Pretender, 'Bonnie Prince Charlie', has a tenuous connection with golf, as in his last sad days in Rome, abandoned without hope, he is said to have whiled away the time hitting a few shots in the Borghese Gardens.* During his campaign to seize the throne of England in 1745, Prince Charles Edward was involved with the surgeon, John Rattray, the champion golfer of Edinburgh who had won the Silver Club competition in 1744 and again in 1745. Rattray was called out in the early hours of 22 September 1745 to tend the wounded after the battle of Prestonpans, in which the Hanoverian troops under General Cope had been worsted. Rattray followed the White Cockade to Derby and stayed with the Jacobites through their dismal retreat back to Scotland. He was at the disastrous battle of Culloden in April 1746 and was captured. It is said that he was saved from the fate of so many of the Prince's supporters at the hands of Cumberland 'The Butcher' by the intervention of a fellow-member of the golf club, Duncan Forbes of Culloden, who held the important post of Lord President of the Court of Sessions and who had gone to the Highlands to try to stop the rebellion.

In the years of the Hanoverian kings nothing was heard of golf in the reigns of the

* Robert Browning, *A History of Golf* (London: Dent, 1955).

Prince Leopold (1853–1886), captain of the Royal and Ancient, 1876

four Georges, but William IV, who came to the throne in 1830, was certainly a benefactor to golf, even if he was not a player. In 1833 he granted the royal title to the Perth Golfing Society and in 1834 to the St Andrews Club, to whom in 1837 he presented a gold medal. This was followed by the presentation of another medal to the Royal and Ancient Golf Club of St Andrews, as it had become, by the Sailor King's widow, Queen Adelaide.

Queen Victoria followed her uncle as Patron of the R & A, Prince Edward, later King Edward VII, became Captain in 1863 and the youngest son of Queen Victoria, Prince Leopold, Duke of Albany, became Captain in 1876.

King Edward VII is said to have been introduced to golf at Musselburgh when he was at Edinburgh University as Prince of Wales, and later in life and when he came to the throne he enjoyed a mild form of the game. He certainly was a supporter of golf as Patron of several clubs and ready giver of the royal title. King Edward's younger brother, the Duke of Connaught, was a royal patron of golf, though he does not seem to have been conspicuous as a player. A good story about the Duke of Connaught as a golfer comes from Ireland. The centenary publication of the (Royal) Curragh Golf Club reports that Lionel Hewson, a Captain in the South Irish Horse, was told off to play the old Duke, then (1904) Commander of the Forces in Ireland: 'at the first green, I was six inches from the hole and he was ten yards. He remarked "I always count 2 on greens and thus avoid putting." ' Early in 1901, when he had become King, Edward VII is shown in a suit of plus-fours in the Golfing Annual for

Edward VII (1841–1910)

1900–1. He is reported as having played at Cannes with another royal golfer, Grand Duke Michael of Russia, and also at Homburg, where it was said: 'He is good at putting, and his lack of skill at other parts of the game does not prevent him from being extremely fond of it, and thinking it a very useful addition to the cure.' Another report claimed that 'he "has secured an excellent style" '. His caddie at Musselburgh, Tom Brown, whose son became Open Champion, is said to have cautioned Prince Edward for pushing rather than striking a putt. Warned to mind his tongue when addressing royalty, Tom, the good blunt Scot, replied: 'His Royal Highness maun learn, for if he did that in a match, he would lose it.' Sir Frederick Ponsonby in his *Recollections of Three Reigns*, gives a description of Edward VII's golf which is too good to paraphrase or summarize, as follows:

> At Sandringham* the King ordered a golf-links to be made in the Park: the putting-greens were good though small and the fair-ways were properly mown, but there were no bunkers. To remedy this the agent, Mr Frank Beck, had placed wicker hurdles to indicate the places where the bunkers would eventually be dug. He argued that they could easily be moved to any position that the King eventually decided upon. This was perfectly sound in theory, but in practice it worked out very badly.

* There was also a private golf course of sorts in the royal grounds of Osborne in the Isle of Wight.

The Duke of Connaught, brother of Edward VII

The first match we had on these links was the King and I playing the same ball against Seymour Fortescue. Nature had not made the King's figure suitable for driving a long ball, but he fancied himself at approaching and putting. Having blinked at the hurdles on the right and left of the fairway, the King proceeded to drive off and of course hit those on the right. The agent, who had come out to see whether the sites for the bunkers were right, looked horrified, but the King merely said 'What a silly place to put a bunker! See that this is altered to-morrow; have them put much more to the right and further off the tee.'

Every other hole the same thing happened, and the King got louder and louder in his denunciation of the stupidity of the person who had placed the hurdles, while the agent took copious notes, but not being a golfer himself he had left the whole thing to the head gardener. However, as Seymour Fortescue kept on driving into the long grass we had quite a good game, and as the King did a very good approach shot at the eighth hole and sank a long putt at the ninth (we played only nine holes), we won on the last green and he quite recovered his temper.

The second day we played he took the even holes and of course drove into the hurdles again, when precisely the same thing happened and he ordered the hurdles to be moved. The third day was the most unnerving for the agent, because the hurdles at all the holes had been moved to different spots indicated by the King. The agent had taken the precaution of bringing out two men to move the hurdles anywhere. Again after viewing the hurdles distastefully the King never failed to drive into them and, in a voice of thunder, asked who had been stupid enough to place them there. When the agent replied by reading out his notes, which proved that it was the King himself who had selected the spot, the King exploded with rage and ordered all the hurdles to be taken away. This was done and orders were given to the head gardener to make proper bunkers. But unfortunately he knew little about this, and the following year erected only two bunkers on the nine holes and made them like fortifications.

On one occasion I proposed to the King to get the professional over from Hunstanton to make a fourth, and I thought that he would be able to get the King over the ground. It was, however, not altogether a success to begin with, as the professional was so nervous that he made all sorts of bad strokes. He wanted to play the game of his life and developed a terrible hook on his drives. The King, who had to play the second shot out of a bush, or out of long grass, cursed him freely, which made him worse. Then he made a mess of his short game and couldn't putt at all, with the result that Seymour Fortescue and I won very easily.

On the way back to the house the King said that quite obviously the man was a very bad player and that no doubt I had selected him because I knew that I could beat him easily. As a matter of fact, the man could give me a stroke a hole any day.

I was so sorry for the professional that I sent him word that I would play him before breakfast the following morning. I explained to him that it was not necessary to play a super game. I had a handicap of nine and Fortescue of fifteen, so that all he had to do was to go straight and give the King a chance of doing well at the short game. The poor man was, however, still so nervous that he couldn't play at all the first three holes, but I got him to tell me some of his triumphs at golf, and he forgot his bad play with the King and settled down to his ordinary game. When the King came out to play at 11.30 he played beautifully and had quite got over his nervousness.

In the afternoon Queen Alexandra and I played against Princess Victoria and Francis Knollys. The Queen seemed to confuse it with hockey and was under the impression that one had to prevent the opponent putting the ball in the hole. This usually ended by a scrimmage on the green. She also thought that the person who got into the hole first won it, and asked me to hurry up and run between the strokes. It was

> very good fun, and we all laughed. Francis Knollys always played in a square-shaped billycock hat and a London tail coat, and hit so hard that his hat almost invariably fell off.

It seems that in the next royal generation (the children of Edward VII), the Duke of Clarence, who died young, was not a golfer but the Duke of York, later King George V, took a limited interest in the game. While he was still Prince of Wales he is reported as playing at Windsor with Ben Sayers, the North Berwick professional, and also as playing at Deal just before he became King. The Duchess of York, later Queen Mary, was reported as having had lessons in Dublin from George, the brother of Ben Sayers. Certainly King Edward's eldest daughter, Princess Royal and Duchess of Fife, was a strong supporter and a player of the game.

George V's sons were golfers, the keenest being Edward, Prince of Wales, later Edward VIII. He played a lot of golf throughout his life but never very well, although he worked hard at his game and reached the final of the Parliamentary Handicap in 1933. Frances Donaldson in her biography of Edward VIII* quotes Maurice Collis's life of Lady Astor, describing the semi-final:†

* Frances Donaldson, *Edward VIII* (London: Weidenfeld & Nicolson, 1974). † Maurice Collis, *Nancy Astor* (London: Faber & Faber, 1960).

The Duke of Windsor, Governor of the Bahamas, and the Duchess pictured with four British and American Open champions in 1941: Gene Sarazen, Bobby Jones, Walter Hagen and Tommy Armour, with an aide (second left)

The Prince of Wales pictured with Lady Astor (wearing eyeshade) at Walton Heath in 1933 in the Parliamentary Handicap

> Her handicap was twenty, his twelve . . . The match took place at Walton Heath on 5 July 1933 . . . He gave out that he particularly disliked a crowd of spectators, but a huge crowd assembled, as was inevitable because it was not every day that one could watch the Prince of Wales playing a match against Lady Astor in the semi-finals of a famous competition. The Prince was very nervous. He drove well, but his putting got worse until on one green he took four. Just before the turn he was two down and seemed to be going to pieces. Lady Astor, who did not want to beat the heir to the throne under such embarrassing circumstances, sought to calm and cheer him. She was always very good at cheering people and in this case was so successful that he pulled himself together. He drew level and when she lost the seventeenth hole, he won the match, two up and one to play. The Prince wore a blue check shirt, grey plus-fours, check stockings and black-and-white shoes.

The Prince of Wales had the misfortune to hit a poor shot when playing himself in as Captain of the Royal and Ancient in 1922. The expectant caddies waiting to gather the shot down the fairway were disappointed as,

Top: *The Prince of Wales (in 1922) and* (above) *the Duke of York (1930) playing themselves in as captain of the Royal and Ancient Golf Club*

The Duke of York opening the second public golf course at Richmond in 1925

seeing what had happened, Willie Petrie dashed out of Gourlay's club-making shop and retrieved the ball and the reward. When the Duke of York, later King George VI, played himself in in 1930, the caddies, expecting a similar performance, stood, it was reported, 'disloyally close to the tee', whereupon the Duke hit a very good shot of some 200 yards and had the last laugh. The third golfer brother, the Duke of Kent, who was killed on active service in World War II, became Captain of the R & A in 1937. Alas he hit an indifferent shot. All three of the Princes played in the St Andrews Autumn Medal after becoming Captain.

In foreign parts, King Leopold II of the Belgians supported the game by granting royal status; so did his son King Albert, while Leopold III was a very fair player. Currently King Baudouin of the Belgians is said to play well. The Spanish royal family, particularly Don Juan, father of the present King of Spain, has shown interest, while King Hassan of Morocco is a real addict.

King George VI, a spectator at the Open Championship at Muirfield in 1948, won by Henry Cotton

CHAPTER 2

Early clubs in Scotland

As we have seen, golf was well established in Scotland as a pastime as early as the middle of the fifteenth century, if not before. It was three hundred years later that the first groupings of players into societies and clubs began in Scotland; we must rule out the possible date of 1608 for the formation of the Blackheath Club by Scots on the outskirts of London. The dates of formation of the clubs whose pedigree goes back to the eighteenth century are as follows:

1	The Royal Burgess Golfing Society of Edinburgh	1735*
2	The Honourable Company of Edinburgh Golfers	1744
3	Royal & Ancient Golf Club of St Andrews	1754
4	Bruntsfield Links Golfing Society	1761
5	Royal Blackheath Golf Club	1766†
6	Royal Musselburgh Golf Club	1774
7	Royal Aberdeen Golf Club	1780
8	Crail Golfing Society	1786
9	Glasgow Golf Club	1787
10	Dunbar Golf Club	1794
11	Burntisland Golf Club	1797

These clubs and those that followed were formed in order to bring together golfers who were congenial, to arrange competitions – which necessitated making rules for the game – to arrange matches and bets among the members and to dine and wine together. The historian of the Royal Blackheath Club points to a strong Masonic background to these early clubs, and, as Donald Steel has pointed out, the formation of the clubs and societies was an important step as it brought about responsibility and care for the links, which had hitherto been left to the attentions of nature.

None of these early clubs had a private golf course; that came much later in the history of the game. The clubs met and played on public links or common land and had no exclusive rights. They made their club headquarters in a private house or a public house or tavern or in a special building of their own construction alongside the links where they played.

The Edinburgh Burgess Society started life as the Society of Golfers in and about Edinburgh and on occasion as the Edinburgh Golfing Society, becoming in 1787 the Burgess Golfing Society of Edinburgh, with the prefix Royal added in 1929. The club has no written records earlier than 1773, but strong circumstantial evidence from other records, the *Edinburgh Almanac*, puts its origin as 1735, which is now the accepted date. In June 1800 the Town Council of Edinburgh granted to the Burgess a Seal of Cause which made the Society a legal corporation with power to hold property, to sue and to be sued, provided that any of its by-laws or regulations were sanctioned by the Lord Provost, Magistrates and Council of the city, a condition which has been observed to this day. The members played their early golf at Bruntsfield Links with 5 or 6 holes. This is now in the centre of Edinburgh, under the shadow of the Castle. It is still a golf course of sorts today, being

* Direct written evidence for this date does not exist, but circumstantial evidence strongly supports it.

† Certainly older than this, but date unknown; some evidence suggests 'before 1745'.

restricted to pitch and putt play on rather flaccid turf. It is hard to picture the royal golfers at play here in the sixteenth century, but play here they did. As a link with the past, the Golf Tavern is still to be found at Bruntsfield.

With the years Bruntsfield Links became more and more confined by the expanding city and threatened by other activities, so the Burgesses decided to move out to the seaside resort of Musselburgh in 1874 where a 9-hole links had long been established. This links still exists today and is probably the oldest golf-course to be found anywhere in the world.

The Burgesses first made a club house of sorts in the grandstand of the race course at Musselburgh, with refreshments available from Mrs Forman's tavern across the links. This tavern too survives to the present day. Then, after amalgamation with the Musselburgh New Club, which dated from 1867, a fine new golf house was built for the Burgesses in 1875, which served until Musselburgh, which was housing four societies and its own local players, became too crowded. The Burgesses then moved across to a private course and a large new club house at Barnton on the west side of Edinburgh in 1894. One of the attractions of the site at Barnton was its proximity to the new railway station, from which a bell was rung in the club house to signal the imminent departure of the train. It is from here that the Burgesses celebrated in 1985 the first 250th anniversary of any golf club in the world with a long programme of events, including an unprecedented match of 200 players a side with their old friends and neighbours the Bruntsfield Links Golfing Society. It finished with a 4-a-side, 2-ball eightsome match played from the first tee at Bruntsfield to the 18th green at Burgess, which was fixed to finish at 6.00 p.m. in time for the cocktail party for all the players, guests and officials at the Barnton club house. The story of the Burgesses' royal connections comes in the next chapter.

Next in date to the Edinburgh Burgess Society came what is now known as the *Honourable Company of Edinburgh Golfers*, a club of unmatched prestige, with the ownership of one of the most famous if one of the most recent championship links in the rota, at Muirfield. In 1744, the earliest date for which the Honourable Company has any record, the club was known as the Gentlemen Golfers of Edinburgh. It changed its name to the present style in 1795 and was given its Charter from the Magistrates of Edinburgh in 1800. The club was probably in existence before the date claimed, because the City of Edinburgh in that year, 1744, provided a prize for what might be regarded as an Open Championship, and this trophy became the property of the Society in 1765.

That invaluable work *Golf: a Royal and Ancient Game* by Robert Clark, published in 1875, tells us that in 1744 the Magistrates of Edinburgh, having been 'from time to time applied to', authorized their 'Treasurer to cause make a SILVER CLUB not exceeding the value of Fifteen pounds sterling to be played for on Leith Links' by golfers from any part of Great Britain and Ireland (on payment of the equivalent of 25p), and it was also laid down that the city was to be put to no further expense whatever on account of the playing for the Club. They did, however, agree to announce the day of the competition by a parade through the city of the Silver Club heralded by 'Tuck of Drum' and to deliver the trophy to Leith Links on the morning of play. The winner of the Silver Club pocketed the entry money, became the 'Captain of the Golf' and appended a silver ball to the trophy. It was stipulated that he 'should settle and determine under the condition of play then in being all disputes touching Golf among golfers'.

From this competition came the original set of rules for the game, drawn up by the Honourable Company in 1744 for the first playing for the Silver Club. These rules were almost exactly copied by the St Andrews

Club when they instituted their Silver Club competition in 1754. These original 1744 rules were, in modern parlance, as follows:

1. You must Tee your Ball within a Club-length of the Hole.
2. Your Tee must be upon the ground.
3. You are not to change the Ball which you strike off the Tee.
4. You are not allowed to remove Stones, Bones or any Break-club for the sake of playing your ball except upon the fair Green, and that only within a Club-length of your Ball.
5. If your Ball come among Water or any watery filth you are at liberty to take your Ball and bringing it behind the hazard and teeing it, you may play it with any club, and allow your Adversary a stroke for so getting out your Ball.
6. If your Balls be found anywhere touching one another you are to lift the first Ball until you play the last.
7. At holing out you are to play your Ball honestly for the Hole and not to play upon your Adversary's Ball, not lying in your way to the hole.
8. If you should lose your Ball by its being taken up or in any other way, you are to go back to the spot where you struck last and drop another Ball and allow your Adversary a stroke for the misfortune.
9. No man at Holing his Ball is to be allowed to mark his way to the Hole with his Club or anything else.
10. If a Ball is stopped by any person, Horse, Dog or anything else, the Ball so stopped must be played where it lies.
11. If you draw your Club in order to strike and proceed so far in the stroke as to be bringing down your Club – if then your Club shall break in any way it is to be accounted a stroke.
12. He whose Ball lies farthest from the Hole is obliged to play first.
13. Neither Trench, Ditch or Dyke made for the preservation of the Links, nor the Scholars' Holes nor the Soldiers' Lines shall be accounted as a Hazard, but the Ball is to be taken out, Teed and played with any iron Club.

The first winner of the Silver Club in 1744 was the surgeon John Rattray, and he won it again in the following year. Later in 1745, as we have seen, he became involved in the Young Pretender's rebellion.

The Honourable Company first played on common ground at Leith Links. Originally there were five holes here, later increased to seven, with length varying from 414 to 496 yards. The Company's first headquarters at Leith was Lucky Clephan's Inn, later replaced by their own golf house. By 1836 Leith, like Bruntsfield Links later on, became too inconvenient, and the Honourable Company moved out to Musselburgh, building their own club house there. At about this time, the club was going through a bad patch and was more or less in suspension between 1832 and 1835. It was then that the St Andrews Club gained the status of premier club which it has retained ever since. The Honourable Company, however, came back with renewed strength, quit Musselburgh as too crowded and uncomfortable in 1891 and migrated to their own links at Muirfield. What is more they removed as it were their 'share' of the Open Championship from Musselburgh to the new course and organized the Open there in 1892, the first time the championship went to four rounds.

The next club to be formed was at St Andrews in 1754, when 22 noblemen and gentlemen of Fife formed themselves into the *Society of St Andrews Golfers*.

Like the Edinburgh clubs, the St Andrews men played their golf on the local links, to which the public had access as of right, as they do to this day, and have only briefly owned a course of their own. Golf has been played on St Andrews Links, close by the shore which gave us that first dramatic shot of the runners in the film *Chariots of Fire*, for

Severiano Ballesteros, winner of the Open Championship at St Andrews in 1984, pictured with the famous trophy

at least five hundred years and probably longer, and every golfer of distinction from Mary Queen of Scots and her forebears to young Tommy Morris and his father to Bobby Jones and Severiano Ballesteros has played here, and many a hundred thousand more of lesser renown. Five courses there are here now, and half a dozen clubs besides the Society of St Andrews Golfers have formed round these famous links.

The original Society progressed with its usual meeting of local interest, using as its headquarters sometimes Baillie Glass's house, sometimes the Black Bull Tavern and sometimes the Cross Keys Inn. The temporary decline of the Honourable Company in Edinburgh in the 1830s brought up the status of the St Andrews Society, and, as we can read later, King William IV in 1834 granted the royal consent to the title of the Society becoming The Royal and Ancient Golf Club of St Andrews, with himself as Patron.

The members subscribed among themselves for the purchase of a Silver Club in 1754 to be played for for the captaincy of the Club as it is today. Since 1824 the Captain has been elected, but he still plays himself in by hitting a stroke at the fearful hour of 8 a.m. from the 1st tee on the last day of the autumn meetings – followed immediately by the discharge of cannon – and later attaches his silver ball to the trophy, having rewarded the caddie who retrieves the driven ball with a gold sovereign.*

After the North British Railway made the branch from the main line at Leuchars to St Andrews in 1852, the town and the golf attracted many more visitors, and accommodation for the golfers became a problem. Joint action with the Union Club in the town, whose premises had been used by R & A members, led in 1854 to the building of the club house which one sees today, though it has undergone numerous alterations since. The Union Club amalgamated with the R & A in 1877.

The Club's prestige and standing continued to grow in the nineteenth century. For example, its reduction of the round of the St Andrews links from 22 holes to 18 set the standard which other golf clubs all over the world have since followed. Before that the round could be anything from 7 holes at Blackheath or Leith to 25 at Montrose. Similarly the sudden surge of interest in the game, taking it far beyond its Scottish home, led to a demand for a uniform set of rules, and the R & A produced a set in 1892 which gained very wide acceptance. More recently the rule-making standing of the R & A, working very closely with the Americans, has stood the test of time.

---

* Those Americans who have reached this high office have given an 'illegal' $5 gold piece.

The third of the R & A's activities today, the organizing and running of the Open and Amateur Championships and other international events, developed over the years and came into force in 1919, although both the championships had originated with other clubs – the Open at Prestwick in 1860 and the Amateur at Hoylake in 1885. Recognition of the R & A as the governing body of the game in the British Isles and the Commonwealth was agreed in 1924.

The Old Course has seen many changes since golf became organized in the middle of the eighteenth century, but today it follows the original layout to a discernible extent, becoming wider, longer and smoother, the biggest change being the introduction of separate holes, on double greens, for the inward and outward nines. The final changes were made in 1913, and, apart from back-tees to cope with the modern ball, the Old Course is much the same now as it was then.

In 1785, on Friday 8 October, a Ball was held 'as usual', this one being notable for the arrival at Cupar, nearby, of the intrepid aeronaut Lunardi, who was blown across the Forth from Edinburgh in his balloon two days before. Lunardi was made much of, being elected to the Club and granted the Freedom of the Town, ending up at the ballroom, where, as he wrote, he found 'upwards of 100 beautiful ladies already assembled'. I must record my regret that the Golf Club Ball has been abandoned. I was lucky enough to be a guest at the Ball in 1925, after having seen Ted Blackwell play himself in as captain with a tremendous swipe. As I wrote afterwards, 'I remember the glamour of the occasion with the scarlet tail coats of the Captains, the plaid sashes of the ladies and kilts swinging in the reels: "Oh the great days in the distance enchanted." '

Next in line was the *Bruntsfield Links Golf Club*, which is believed to date from 1760 or 1761, although no more positive evidence exists than a club minute of 1790 which states that it had been in existence for thirty years.

Vincent Lunardi became a great favourite at St Andrews and was elected to the Club in 1785

At any rate the Club celebrated its centenary in 1861, the Lord Provost of Edinburgh being present.

The *Shell Encyclopedia of Golf* reports a romantic theory that the Bruntsfield Links Club was formed by a number of members of the Edinburgh Burgesses who, having been supporters of Prince Charles Edward in the '45, did not relish drinking the health of King George and decided to break away. Be that as it may, the two clubs have long been harmonious neighbours, first at Bruntsfield Links, where they combined from time to time to defeat damaging or encroaching attempts to interfere with golf, then in sharing the use of Musselburgh Links and, finally, as neighbours in western Edinburgh, where the Bruntsfield Club is now lodged hard by the Burgesses at Davidson's Mains at Barnton. The Bruntsfield Links Club has the distinction of having provided the first individual open tournament champion, Robert Chambers, the famous publisher, who as a young man won the open meeting at St Andrews in 1858. He was the youngest player in a field of twenty-eight and beat the oldest, D. Wallace, in the final.*

The Bruntsfield Links Club moved out to Musselburgh in 1874 and built themselves a club house which served until 1898, when they followed the example of the Honourable Company, the Burgesses and the Royal Musselburgh Club itself and moved to less crowded golf on their own private course.

The Royal Musselburgh Golf Club was not formed until 1774, although golf had been played on the little links there for two or three hundred years. Although no written records exist earlier than 1784, the club possesses a cup dating from 1774 to which the winners have attached medals. This then is the accepted date, though one reference suggests that the club was in existence in 1760. Like the other clubs, Musselburgh – it became Royal in 1876 – had its own club house which it used until 1925, when it too abandoned its old golfing grounds and moved out to Prestongrange House at Prestonpans further along the coast, where James Braid laid out a fine park course. A new layout by Mungo Park was made in 1939.

The old Musselburgh Links consisted of 7 holes; an 8th was added in 1832 and a 9th shortly afterwards. I am delighted to be able to include in the colour section a fine plan of Musselburgh Links drawn by Mr T. M. Lamb, through the good offices of Mr Hastie. Old Musselburgh, which is open to the public to play to this day, housed the Open Championship six times between 1874 and 1889. The present 2nd hole, the 'Graves', is so called because the dead Scottish soldiers from the Battle of Pinkie in 1547 are buried there. An unusual competition at the old links was a prize offered to the local fishwives, a formidable body of ladies.

Like others, the club had periods of inactivity when the Cup was not competed for, from 1797 to 1807, from 1812 to 1827, from 1848 to 1852 and finally from 1859 to 1869, but otherwise the Cup has been played for to this day and holds an honoured place among the Club's trophies and possessions, among which are two priceless golf-clubs, one of which, we are told, has been owned by King James II when he was Duke of York in 1682. Another rare trophy is a hole-cutter dated 1774, with the 4¼-inch diameter which rules today.

A crisis developed in Royal Musselburgh's affairs in 1954, when the owners wanted to sell the land which the Club had so far rented. The Club could not raise the £6000 needed, but the Coal Industry Social Welfare Organisation, which had an interest in providing amenities for the coal-miners working in the nearby pits, came to the rescue and for £8000 bought the entire property. Today, we were told, it is valued at £1,650,000. With a miners' social club joining forces, the joint affair is now flourishing, with 750 members of whom about 15%, we are told, are miners or ex-miners. Once there were 23 pits near here, today only two survive in active use.

Prestongrange House is a Scots baronial mansion with a massive tower, making it one of the most impressive club houses in the country. Ownership of the Prestongrange estate can be traced back to 1165. From 1185 the monks of Newbattle held it for 400 years until the Reformation. The Kerr family owned it under the title of Lord Lothian; thence it passed through several Lords Pres tongrange to the Grand-Suttie family. The progress of such ownership to a coal-miners' welfare society is a pleasing, if surprising, sign of the times.

Last in this chapter we can have a look at the *Royal Aberdeen Golf Club*, whose origin goes back to 1780 when the Society of

* Once again the invaluable Robert Browning.

The 18th green at Royal Musselburgh

Golfers of Aberdeen was founded; it emerged as the Aberdeen Golf Club in 1815, with the royal title added in 1903. The continuity linking Society and Club is shown by the 1780 ballot box and the 1783 President's chair in use today which both passed from the one to the other.

Play was originally at Aberdeen Links, a piece of common land owned by the city between the rivers Don and Dee, on which golf was played at least as early as 1565 and almost certainly earlier. A club house was built by the links in 1866, and in 1872 Prince Leopold, Duke of Albany, became Patron of the club until he died in 1884. In 1873 he presented a cup which is played for at the spring meeting each year.

By 1888 the links had become overcrowded and subject to damage by footballers, so the club leased some fresh links land at Balgownie, north of the river Don, and laid out its own course at a cost of £100. At first the Bridge of Don Hotel was used as a club house, but by 1890 the Club's own premises were available. In 1903 the royal title was granted – a separate honour from the royal Patronage of Prince Leopold in the earlier years.

CHAPTER 3

Royal Golf Clubs in Scotland

There are ten recognized golf clubs in Scotland which bear the royal title, with the following dates:

	Club	Date formed	Date of royal title
1	Royal Perth Golfing Society	1824	1833
2	Royal and Ancient Golf Club of St Andrews	1754	1834
3	Royal Montrose, formerly Royal Albert	1810/1864	1845
4	Royal Musselburgh	1774	1876
5	Royal Aberdeen	1780	1903
6	Royal Dornoch	1877	1906
7	Duff House Royal	1871/1909	1923
8	Royal Tarlair	1926	1926
9	Royal Burgess Golfing Society of Edinburgh	1735	1929
10	Royal Troon	1878	1978

There was also at one time the royal household club on Deeside, the Royal Craggan, and there is the thriving club of the same sort on the royal estate at Balmoral today.

ROYAL PERTH GOLFING SOCIETY

Golf in Perth goes back at least 400 years in written record, and one can add another century to this with fair certainty. For example, we read in the Perth Kirk Session records the following:

> Nov 19 1599 – John Gardiner, James Bowman, Laurence Chalmers and Laurence Cuthbert confessed that they were playing at the golf on the North Inch at the time of the afternoon preaching on the Sabbath. The Session rebuked them and admonished them to resort to the hearing of the word diligently on the Sabbath in time coming which they promised to do.

King James VI learned to play golf at Perth on the North Inch course or the South Inch, both of which courses survive to this day.

The date of the formation of the Club, first known as the Perth Golfing Society, is obscure, but the first minute available is dated 5 April 1824. The Society acquired the usual Silver Club, and gold and silver medals were put up for competition at the spring and autumn meetings in the early days. In 1833 the idea of inviting King William IV to become Patron of the Society was accepted, no doubt because the King bore one of the royal titles of his House, Duke of St Andrews. Quoting from the club's official history:

> At a meeting of the Council on the ninth day of August, 1833, the Right Honourable Lord Kinnaird, Captain of the Club, presiding, the chairman intimated to the meeting that he had been recently in London, when he took the opportunity of addressing a letter to His Majesty King William the Fourth, soliciting His Majesty to become the Patron of the Society, and to grant his permission for styling it in future, the 'Royal Perth Golfing Society',

King William IV (1765–1837) and Queen Adelaide, who gave the royal title to Perth and the Royal and Ancient

and wearing an appropriate button, a drawing of which he had submitted to the King; to which application His Majesty was graciously pleased to accede, in a letter transmitted to his Lordship by Sir Herbert Taylor, the tenor of which follows:-

'Windsor Castle,
June 4, 1833

My dear Lord,

I have had the honour to submit to the King your Lordship's letter and the enclosed drawing of the button of the Perth Golfing Society, and I am directed to acquaint you that His Majesty approves the button, and to repeat to your Lordship what He had already stated to you verbally, that His Majesty has great pleasure in meeting the wish of the Society that it should be styled Royal and placed under his patronage.

I have the honour to be, my Dear Lord,
Your Lordship's obedient humble servant,
H. Taylor

The Right Honble.
Lord Kinnaird
etc., etc.

The meeting having received this gratifying communication from his Lordship, it was moved by Pat G. Stewart, Esq., and carried unanimously, that the best thanks of the Society were due to Lord Kinnaird for the very great interest he had uniformly taken in the Society's affairs, since he became connected with it, and particularly for this distinguished mark of his Lordship's attention, in having procured the Royal patronage for this Society, an honour of which no other Golfing Society in Britain can boast.

Thereafter his Lordship presented to the Society a quantity of buttons with the device approved of by His Majesty, for the use of the members, when it was agreed that these should be worn upon a blue dress coat at all convivial meetings of the Society.

The meeting instructed the Secretary to get Sir Herbert Taylor's letter neatly framed, and placed beside the other insignia of the Society, and he is also instructed to intimate this day's proceedings to the members.'*

The royal patronage of the Perth Society, to be known finally as the Royal Perth Golfing Society and County and City Club, has continued: Queen Victoria succeeded her uncle as Patroness, followed by King Edward VII, George V, Edward VIII, George VI and, at the moment, the Duke of Edinburgh.

A delightful picture of golf and club life from 150 years ago is given in the Society's history:

A graphic account of the dinner of the Perth Royal Golfing Society at which His Grace the Duke of Buccleuch presided as Captain, has been preserved in the diary of a young barrister who was a guest on the occasion.

He had come on a visit, along with his relatives, Sir Alexander and Lady Dickson, to Mr Archibald Turnbull of Bellwood, in the autumn of 1837 . . .

* The Rev. T. D. Miller, *History of the Royal Perth Society* (Perth: The Mungo Press Ltd, 1935).

This is how the proceedings of the morning and evening struck 'a stranger':-

'We arrived from Dundee at six o'clock in the morning on a visit to Mr Archie Turnbull, of Bellwood House, Perth, a fine specimen of a bachelor's mansion. At breakfast we were joined by Major Guthrie and Mr Moncrieff, W.S., and at noon, we descended to the North Inch to see the game of golf played by members of the Royal Perth Golfing Society, for a gold medal. As to the Society, the late King [William IV] extended his patronage to them and made them a Royal Society. The holes are situated round the Inch, and to play the whole game takes about an hour and a half; the holes are about 300 or 400 yards apart and in every variety of direction.

A boy is stationed at each hole to mark its exact situation, to guide the striker. When the ball is struck with force to impel it forward as far as possible, it is called "driving", and when it has been driven near the hole, so that only a small force and skilful management are required to send it into the hole, it is called "putting". There were about a dozen competitors for the medal, all dressed in their uniform coat, scarlet with black collar and an appropriate club button. They played in pairs, each pair waiting till the other had advanced a hole's length, and a person accompanied each pair to mark the number of strokes taken between each hole.

The hole from whence the start is made is the last one, at which stood the president of the club, Colonel Belshes of Invermay, a stately, pompous, but very gentlemanly man, who received the lists from the markers as they finished; and when all had arrived successfully at the last hole, comparing the lists, he declared Captain Hope Grant (afterwards Sir Hope Grant), 9th Lancers, aide-de-camp to Lord Greenock, the successful man.

Mr Turnbull took me to the annual dinner given by the Society in the County Hall, the Duke of Buccleuch, captain of the Society, in the chair, supported by Sir John Richardson of Pitfour on the right, and Sir Patrick Murray Thriepland on the left, Colonel Belshes, the president of the club, officiating as croupier to the Duke. About 120 sat down to dinner, three tables lengthways and one across, in the centre of which sat His Grace of Buccleuch. After dinner the usual loyal toasts, and different golfing clubs were drunk; Edinburgh is the oldest, St Andrews second, and Perth third. The Duke's health was then proposed by Colonel Belshes and drunk with great applause.

The Duke stated in his speech his intention of giving the Society a gold medal to be played for annually in addition to the club one, and of applying to the proper quarter to get the Queen to extend her patronage to the Society. It is composed of captain, president and council.

The Duke then called upon the victor of the day, Captain Grant, to receive the reward of his merits, and put the gold medal, attached to a ribbon, round his neck amidst great applause. The newly-elected members, amongst whom was Major Wemyss, better known by the sobriquet of "Flash Jim", were called upon to do homage and fealty to their superior, His Grace, the captain. This ceremony consists in kissing, separately, two rows of silver balls which are attached to the handle part of a massive silver golf club. This club is held by the captain while the kissing ceremony lasts. It is hollow, and it was originally the custom for each newly-elected member to empty it after it had been filled with wine, but this custom is now "more honoured in the breach than in the observance".

After divers other toasts had been given, and glees sung by the professional vocalist, and Scotch tunes played by the fiddlers, who operated in the orchestra, the Duke proposed the health of the strangers, of whom there were but four or five present. My horror was great when nobody rose to return thanks, and, finding divers pairs of eyes directed to me, in mute expectation of the outpouring of a stream of eloquence, I made an effort, and sprang up on my legs, screwing my courage to the sticking point, and after thanking my Lord Duke and gentlemen for the honour, etc., and, eulogising the "noble game of golf" (which, by the bye, I think is a very stupid game), I resumed my seat, and began to wonder whether or not I had made a fool of myself.'

Royal Perth has always played its golf on the course on the North Inch and still does, as is reported in *Play the Best Courses*:*

> Today there are eighteen holes on the North Inch, together with football and hockey fields, with a total length for the course of 5000 odd yards. There is nothing really to show that it is historic turf. The ground is flat, there are few trees; the river is on one side, with perhaps a man in waders trying for a salmon, and solid citizens' houses on the other.
>
> Various games are played, numerous golfers are on the move and dogs are being exercised; it looks not unlike Clapham Common. The length of the course has varied; in very early days there were only six holes, then nine, and for quite a time ten; thirteen holes next made the round and finally eighteen; the holes have also moved away from the city, which would be easy enough with their simple layout.
>
> The start of the round is dreary in the extreme, flat, featureless and without rough or hazards, three holes up and down the common. As the Rev. T. D. Miller wrote at the turn of the century: 'To a stranger, at the first glance, the Inch seems sadly lacking in hazards. In the park part there is ample scope for the wildest of drives. But it is when we leave the Inch and gain the peninsula that the real sport begins.'
>
> And that is so today, bunkers shrewdly placed, small greens and the proximity of the river, all make for good fun once out beyond the parkland. The holes at the end, the long one-shot fourteenth up to the river's edge, the 369-yard fifteenth all along it with the easy possibility of a hook into it, the short tricky little sixteenth right by the water, all these make good sport. So after a dull start and a dreary eighteenth we find we have enjoyed ourselves more than we expected, but, of course, we have not played the actual *holes* which King James VI played, but have played on the *ground* where he and his predecessors played.
>
> The holes must have altered many times, but no matter, it is good to have visited such an historic spot. After all, the great players of a hundred and more years ago all competed here: Young Tom, Allan Robertson, Willie Park, and the most famous of the players in the town, Bob Andrews named 'The Rook'.

By the way, the first honorary member of the Society was Mr Charles Robertson, Preacher of the Gospel, afterwards known as 'goufin' Charlie'. *The King James VI Golf Club*, which occupies the whole South Inch island in the Tay at Perth, deserves a place here, although it is not a royal club in the true sense. It was formed in 1858 and so antedates all clubs in England except Blackheath and Old Manchester; it is named in honour of the King, who learned his golf in Scotland and later gave orders to allow Sunday play for churchgoers after service.

THE ROYAL AND ANCIENT GOLF CLUB OF ST ANDREWS

So much has been written about St Andrews – and it is so widely available as to be almost common knowledge – that this account will be largely limited to the acquisition of the royal title.

In H. S. C. Everard's history of the Club, published in 1907 by Blackwood & Son, we read:

> Engrossed in the minutes are copies of the letters which passed between Major Murray Belshes* and Sir Herbert Taylor, private

* Peter Allen, *Play the Best Courses* (London: Stanley Paul, 1973 and 1987).

* President of the Society and later its Captain.

secretary to his Majesty King William IV. These letters are six in number, and disclose the circumstances under which his Majesty consented to become patron of the Club, and to bestow upon it the designation of 'Royal and Ancient'.

Letter No. 1, 9th January 1834, asks Sir Herbert respectfully to communicate to the King the earnest wish of the members that, as his Majesty was Duke of St Andrews, he would be graciously pleased to become patron of the Club. Also, since the Club was, with the exception of the Edinburgh Club, the oldest in Scotland, that his Majesty would permit it to be styled Royal and Ancient.

No. 2, from Sir Herbert, announces that the King approves of the designation 'Royal and Ancient', but regrets that he cannot become its patron; for ever since his Majesty's accession to the throne he has been compelled to decline similar requests from other societies, and to give any preference, however well merited, might prove embarrassing.

In No. 3, Major Murray Belshes is peculiarly gratified to learn that his Majesty has been pleased to accede to that request of the members, in so far as to approve of the Society being styled Royal and Ancient, but is very sorry to find that circumstances prevented his Majesty becoming patron of the Club. Major Murray Belshes had not been aware of the rule laid down by his Majesty, and, indeed, would not have ventured to make the request at all, had it not been for the fact that Lord Kinnaird had informed him that his Majesty had recently consented to become patron of the Perth Society, and to approve of its being styled 'Royal'. That being the case, and under the peculiar circumstances of his Majesty being Duke of St Andrews, it appeared to Major Murray Belshes that if any preference were to be given, the Golf Club of St Andrews, of the two, was perhaps the better entitled to it, not only from the above circumstances, but from its being nearly a century older, and from its members being entirely composed of a great portion of the nobility and gentry of Scotland. Many of these were in different quarters of the world, and though most gratifying to every member of the Club, yet to those far distant from their native land such a mark of honourable distinction conferred upon them by their sovereign would be received with feelings of the deepest gratitude and pleasure.

By means of these forcible arguments, the pertinacious Major succeeded in carrying his point, for in No. 4 Sir Herbert Taylor admits that the precedent cited had escaped his Majesty's recollection. His Majesty therefore acquiesced in the wish of the Club that he should become its patron, as being Duke of St Andrews. The remaining letters notify the King's decision to the secretary of the Club, for the information of the members.

The royal Patron did the Club proud, as he presented them with a Gold Medal and Green Riband in 1837, with the inscription 'Presented by His Majesty King William the Fourth to the Royal and Ancient Golph Club of St Andrews'. After his death, his widow, Queen Adelaide, as Duchess of St Andrews, became Patroness and gave the Club the Royal Adelaide Medal, in 1838. The King's Gold Medal is today the chief award of the club at the Autumn Meeting, and Queen Adelaide's Medal is the captain's symbol of office and worn by him on all formal occasions.

In 1863 the Prince of Wales became Captain of the R & A and was excused the ordeal of playing himself in, but when in September 1876 the youngest son of Queen Victoria, Prince Leopold, Duke of Albany, became Captain it was reported 'His Royal Highness struck the ball very fairly sending it over the heads of the spectators.' When he died in 1884 a message of sympathy was sent to the Queen, ending with these words:

> We recall with feelings of painful interest the visits of his Royal Highness in 1876 and 1877, when he officiated as Captain of our Royal and Ancient Club, and endeared himself to all its

Caddies scramble for the ball in the early 1900s at St Andrews after the captain has played himself in

> members by the happy courtesy and kindness with which he discharged all the duties of the office. It touches us to think that a career which then seemed so bright and promising has been suddenly closed, to the great grief of your Majesty and the loss of the country which had begun to reap the benefits of his Royal Highness's rare gifts and culture.

When King Edward VII's accession was proclaimed in the Burgh of St Andrews the R & A was represented at the ceremony, the Club Officer, Nicholas Robb, carrying the Silver Clubs draped in crêpe and the Professional, Old Tom Morris, now advanced in years, carrying with some effort the Silver Putter.

It is perhaps of interest to note that the first national golf championship ever played was held at St Andrews on 29, 30 and 31 July 1857, although the idea had come from the Prestwick Club. The results were these:

First Round

Royal Blackheath beat Royal Perth by 8 holes
Edinburgh Burgess beat Montrose Royal Albert by 12 holes
Edinburgh Bruntsfield beat Prestwick by 3 holes
Royal & Ancient beat Dirleton Castle by 10 holes
Innerleven beat Musselburgh by 2 holes
North Berwick, a bye
The Honourable Company of Edinburgh Golfers and Panmure failed to turn up and scratched

Second Round

Royal Blackheath beat Innerleven by 12 holes
Edinburgh Burgess and Edinburgh Bruntsfield halved
Royal & Ancient beat North Berwick by 4 holes

Third Round

Royal Blackheath beat Edinburgh Bruntsfield by 6 holes
Royal & Ancient beat Edinburgh Burgess by 3 holes

Final

Royal Blackheath beat Royal & Ancient by 7 holes

Thus the fine silver claret jug came south, though there is no record of whether the winning pair played each other for the trophy and the champion's title. Next year a singles tournament was played at St Andrews, and, as we have seen, the youngest entrant, Chambers, beat the oldest, Wallace, in the final.

The Prince of Wales with William Petrie, the caddie who secured the ball after the Prince had driven in as captain of the Royal and Ancient Club in 1922

Bobby Jones, who led the American team to victory in the Walker Cup match at St Andrews in 1926

THE ROYAL MONTROSE GOLF CLUB (Formerly the Montrose Royal Albert Golf Club)

As we know, the game of golf in Scotland was established long before any clubs were formed and at Montrose this is how things developed. Golf here as a sport for all goes back for hundreds of years; the links continued in use and clubs were organized by men of like tastes here as elsewhere in eastern Scotland.

In 1810 the Montrose Golf Club was formed, to be followed later by other clubs, all of which used the links that lie between the town and the sea. In January 1843 a meeting of members of the Club was held at which the following minute was recorded:

Jack Nicklaus celebrates his win in the British Open at St Andrews in 1978

The meeting considering that it would be very gratifying if the Club could procure the Royal Authority so as to enable them to rank in the same state as the Club at Perth and other Golfing Societies – Resolved to present a dutiful and loyal address to Prince Albert on the birth of the Princess and to remit to the Captain and Council to prepare and transmit the proper address and to use the other measures necessary for attaining the object in view.

Next we find for 15 April 1845 this minute, reporting a letter sent to Mr Gladstone, the Prime Minister:

The honour to which the club aspires is to obtain the gracious consent of his Royal Highness that it shall in future be styled 'The Montrose Royal Albert Golf Club'. The club has existed under its present designation for many years and is composed of most of the respectable inhabitants of this Town. You are probably aware that we possess a Golf ground unequalled by any in Scotland.*

The Golf clubs at St Andrews and Perth have both been honoured by being allowed the title of Royal. The Montrose Club does not pretend to rank so high as the former but they consider themselves on an equality with the latter and they therefore hope their Claim may be treated with equal consideration as theirs was.

If you shall be so kind as to consent to receive our application and present it and if His Royal Highness shall be so gracious as to confer this honour of patronizing our Club, it will be an additional satisfaction to us that this honour shall be obtained through and towards whom in common with the Public at large the members entertain the deepest feelings of respect. They have the honour to be Sir etc. etc.

The Captain called the attention of the meeting to Mr Gladstone's reply, which he now produced, and which the Secretary was instructed to insert in this minute as follows:

11th April 1845 13 Carlton House Terrace
Sir
I have the pleasure to inform you that through Mr Anson I have brought under the notice of His Royal Highness The Prince Albert the wish of the Montrose Golf Club communicated to me in your letter of the 4th and that the Prince has graciously acceded to it without putting you to the trouble of any more formal communication so that the Club is at liberty to assume its associated designation forthwith. I have the honour to be Sir your very faithful servant.

(Signed) W. E. Gladstone

* At that time 17 holes!

In their thanks to the Prime Minister for bringing off their wish to be 'Royal' the club invited him to become an honorary member.

Not content with obtaining the royal title and Prince Albert's patronage, the club in September 1848 wrote a letter of almost inconceivable pomposity asking if an Address to be presented to the Prince who was then on holiday in Balmoral would be acceptable. The phrases to be put before Prince Albert include such gems as:

> beg with deepest respect to approach your Royal Highness through the medium of this address and to convey to you the expression of our loyal and at the same time our heartfelt congratulations on the auspicious visit of Her Majesty and your Royal Highness to this portion of Her Majesty's ancient Kingdom of Scotland.
>
> We embrace the opportunity of respectfully expressing our grateful thanks to your Royal Highness for your gracious condescension in permitting us to use your Royal title in the designation of our ancient club and we humbly thank your Royal Highness for the continuance you have thus extended to an ancient and National sport in which many of the Kings of Scotland have been known to participate with enthusiastic pleasure . . .

and so on and so on. It is not surprising that the Prince, who we have no reason to suppose was the least interested in golf, turned down this request. He was probably bored with the Club's refusal (in the words of Mr George Strachan, the club's historian, who has provided us with such a rich store of information) to take 'yes' for an answer. At any rate the Prince's Secretary said that HRH had accepted the Address but did not want a personal presentation while he was at Balmoral and sent his thanks to the members of the Club.

In 1863, on the death of their Patron, the Montrose Royal Albert Club invited the Prince of Wales to become Patron of the Club in place of 'his lamented father' and the Prince of Wales agreed.

Coming now to more modern times, we find that until recently there have been four clubs, with their own club houses near the two courses on the links. In 1986 the Royal Albert Club merged with the Victoria Club, which had been formed in 1864, and the last Captain of the Royal Albert Club, Mr J. A. C. Clarke, wrote petitioning the Patron of the Royal Albert, the Duke of Edinburgh, to allow the name of the new club to be the Royal Montrose Golf Club. This was agreed in the following letter from Brigadier Clive Robertson at Buckingham Palace:

> Dear Mr Clarke
>
> Thank you for your letter of 13th December 1985 in which you seek the Duke of Edinburgh's patronage to be transferred to the new merged Golf Club.
>
> I am pleased to say that His Royal Highness has agreed to continue his patronage if the name is changed. Perhaps you could keep me informed as to the progress of the merger.
>
> Yours sincerely
>
> Clive Robertson

The Royal Albert Club had long had a close relationship with the Royal Blackheath Club, with a match each year home and away.

The No. 1 course at Montrose is comparatively new; a much older layout was originally used to the west with an impressive round of 25 holes. The present medal course is an excellent links not too well known outside Scotland, but the Scottish Professional Championship has been held here. The outward 9 is laid out, as it were, in the foothills of the coastal dunes and provides links golf at its most typical, with narrow, rolling, lumpy fairways, greens in dells or on plateaux provided by nature and supplemented by man with a liberal sprinkling of pot bunkers. The inward 9 is on much flatter ground, and as so often happens, is the longer and harder half. There are only three par-3s, one of great quality and menace and one of almost extreme length and difficulty.

ROYAL MUSSELBURGH GOLF CLUB

As we have seen, the Club at Musselburgh dates from 1774 and the royal title came just over a century later.

Prince Arthur, Duke of Connaught, the next to youngest son of Queen Victoria, granted the royal title in 1876 and remained Patron until he died in 1942. The Duke of Connaught's life provides one of those exceptionally long links with the past which I always find diverting. He was born in 1850, just in time to be the godchild of the Duke of Wellington, who had been born in 1769 and died in 1852; the span of the two lives was thus 173 years. The Duke of Connaught's son, Prince Arthur of Connaught, who died in 1938, was Honorary Vice-President from 1912. In 1897 the Connaught Cup was handed to the President of the Club, Sir William Hope, at a ceremony at which the Grand Duke Michael of Russia, who was a keen golfer, had been made an honorary member.

Previous pages have shown that Musselburgh Links at the end of the nineteenth century must have been an exceptionally busy place, with half a dozen clubs all using the 9 holes. In order to keep the course in proper order, the four senior clubs there formed the Green Committee in 1877, ending the 100 years of control by the Musselburgh Club itself.

The Open Championship was started by the Prestwick Club in 1860 and was played there for eleven years. Old Tom Morris from St Andrews won four of these Championships, old Willie Park of Musselburgh won three, and then young Tom Morris won three times in a row and so took the prize of the Belt outright. There was a gap of a year while Prestwick, St Andrews and the Honourable Company conferred, after which it was agreed that the Open would be held in rotation at the links of the three clubs. Young Tom won again in 1872 at Prestwick with the amazing score of 149 for 36 holes; his average round of 74½ was not beaten for over thirty years. Then, alas, the greatest player of his day died, aged only twenty-four.

Musselburgh's turn to have the Open first came in 1874, when Mungo Park, one of the famous golfing family of the town, won, then again in 1877, 1880 and 1883, 1886 and 1889, after which the Honourable Company moved, taking the Championship with them, away from Musselburgh to Muirfield. Willie Fernie's championship in 1883 was notable in that he had a 10 at one hole and then won in a play-off against Bob Ferguson, who had won three times in a row. At the last hole Fernie holed a 'long steal' for a 2 and the title.

Musselburgh was the home of many famous money matches, which were much in fashion in Victorian days. For twenty years Old Willie Park had a standing challenge in *Bell's Life* to play any man in the world for £100 a side. Anyone who thinks that inordinate partisanship by the spectators, such as was seen to a disagreeable extent on the last day of the Open Championship at Muirfield in 1987 and at the Ryder Cup match at the Belfry in 1985, was a new and ugly development should take note of the reputation which Musselburgh supporters had a hundred years ago, 'they damned miners' as Andra Kirkaldy the St Andrews professional called them. In 1882 when Old Willie Park was two up and six to play in a match against Old Tom, Chambers, the publisher and ex-amateur champion, who was refereeing the game, stopped play because spectators were interfering with the balls. Chambers and Morris went into Mrs Forman's pub, and Park, after a wait, said that if Morris would not come out and finish the match he would play on alone and claim the stakes, which he did. J. H. Taylor suffered so badly from such interference in his match with Young Willie Park in 1895 that Harry Vardon in his great challenge match with Young Willie in 1899 refused to play the Scottish half at Mussel-

Mrs Forman's pub at Musselburgh into which Old Tom Morris retired during a match with Willie Park

burgh and they played at North Berwick instead.

It is good that the Musselburgh Links of 9 holes survives to this day, a venerable monument if ever there was one. It now measures 2710 yards with a par of 33, and everybody who loves the game and its ancient origins should pay the £1.20 fee and play it. There are no holes of great distinction, the best perhaps being the 6th, with a drive over a once-big bunker, 'Pandy' (Pandemonium), and a steeply banked two-tier step-green which Young Willie Park, who laid out many courses in the 1890s, copied a number of times: for example, at the 3rd (once the 13th) at Huntercombe and the 8th at Worplesdon.

ROYAL ABERDEEN GOLF CLUB

As we have seen in the chapter dealing with the origins of eighteenth-century Scottish clubs, Royal Aberdeen traces its origins back to 1780; and a huge bicentennial gathering, with representatives of 41 royal clubs, whose display of flags made a brave show, and other friends was held in 1980.

The royal connection began in 1872, when Prince Leopold became the Patron of the Aberdeen Golf Club, a position he held until he died all too young in 1884. Prince Leopold's patronage did not confer the royal title on the club. This was granted by King Edward VII, who also became Patron.

In pursuit of the royal title Colonel James Davidson, the Captain of the Club, wrote in July 1903 to Lord Balfour of Burleigh, the Secretary of State for Scotland, asking him to put before the King the club's petition to use the royal title.

On 10 August 1903 Lord Balfour of Burleigh replied in these terms:

Sir,

I have had the honour to lay before the King the application of the Aberdeen Golf Club, made through you, to use the word Royal in the title of the Club.

I have it in command to inform you that His Majesty was pleased to receive the Petition in the most gracious manner, and to signify His Majesty's pleasure that the Club shall hereafter be known as the 'Royal Aberdeen Golf Club'.

I am,
Sir
Your obedient Servant
(Signed) Balfour of Burleigh

This letter was acknowledged by Colonel Davidson with the grateful thanks of the Club, and the Club members in turn thanked the Captain for his efforts at a special general meeting on 28 August 1903.

The links at Balgownie provides seaside golf at its best, and if it is not as famous as some other Scottish courses it is not from lack of quality. That fine golfer and discriminating critic Sam McKinlay, quoted in *Play the Best Courses*,* gives it high praise. He says:

> I would go so far as to say that there are few courses in these islands with a better, more testing, more picturesque outward nine than Balgownie. It has everything – good two-shot holes, two excellent one-shotters, one two-shotter which is only 'a kick and a spit' but both must be plumb accurate, and a par 5 second hole which must be one of the best long holes in the country.
>
> What adds enormously to the charm of the first half of the course is that the player is never out of sight or sound of the sea except when he is in the valley. Some of the tees stand high on the dunes, overlooking Aberdeen Bay and if you have an eye for the other beauties of nature you may see and hear a raft of eider duck mewing just off the shore or a flight of whooper swans heading north for the Ythan Sanctuary.

Or I might add in these days the clatter of helicopters flighting out to the off-shore oil rigs.

* Peter Allen, *Play the Best Courses* (London: Stanley Paul, 1973 and 1987).

ROYAL DORNOCH

Here again is a place where golf has been played for hundreds of years on open public links land beside the cold North Sea waters up beyond Inverness. Organized golf as a club came late here, as Dornoch Golf Club was not formed until 1877 – but better late than never, for today we have here one of the finest and most famous golf-courses in the world. Much of the fame and quality of Dornoch are due to the work of John Sutherland, who was Secretary for 53 years and no mean golfer at that. Not only did he see that the golf was of the best, but he also promoted the virtues of the old cathedral town and encouraged the emergence of a powerful group of golfers who burst upon the astonished world at the Amateur Championship at Muirfield in 1909 when every one of the favourites, John Ball, Harold Hilton, Jerome Travers from America, Harry Colt the architect, John Low and J. L. C. Jenkins, was knocked out by Dornoch golfers.

Even after that the Dornoch links was not well known except to a discerning few like Roger Wethered and his famous sister and Ernest Holderness, all of them Amateur champions in the 1920s. It was just too far away, only 70 miles from John O'Groats, a sort of Ultima Thule, alluring but unattainable. Now all has changed, and already Dornoch has hosted the Amateur Championship – and the 100th at that. There is almost a cult of Dornoch today, for which we can, I think, thank Herbert Warren Wind, the American writer, such a perceptive observer of golf in Britain and such a charming writer of the game, who described in full in the *New Yorker* magazine his first visit there in 1964.

On a personal note, I had heard so much about Dornoch that it would not have been a surprise if reality had been a disappointment, but for once it was not so, for I found this to be a magnificent links with some of the most beautiful sites for greens on natural plateaux you could imagine. But then

Donald Ross, one of America's most famous golf-course architects, came from Dornoch.

We seem to have strayed away from the royal connection with the club. This can be traced to the friendship of King Edward VII with the Duke of Sutherland and his family, who lived nearby at Dunrobin Castle. John Sutherland said in a speech in 1933: 'In 1906 through the influence of Her Grace the Duchess of Sutherland, Duchess Millicent, one of our very best friends, our club secured the title and dignity of "Royal" from King Edward VII.'

DUFF HOUSE ROYAL GOLF CLUB, BANFF

As in so many places on the Scottish coast, golf was played on the rough links at Banff long before any organized club of golfers was formed. There is one written record of golf here as far back as 1637, when it was reported that 'the last penalty of the law was visited on Franceis Broun' for having stolen some 'golf ballis from the booth of Patrick Shand and selling twa' of them to Thomas Urquhart, servand'. This, I feel, must be the only case known of someone being hanged for stealing golf-balls.

The Banff Golf Club was formed in 1871, and its members continued to share the links close to the sea-shore with non-members, sheep, fishermen's nets and the town washing drying on the whins. At the start the club had fourteen members and the course 8 holes. In the first competition the winning score was 57, but later that same year the record was down to 41. The Club had its ups and downs – once spending a year in abeyance – but by the end of the century it had 'a charming little nine hole course' which was enlarged and improved up to 1914. World War I brought its problems, and after the war the invasion of holiday-makers and their cars on the limited area between the sea and the railway made golf more and more difficult, until, amid controversy, the club decided to amalgamate with its neighbour in Banff, the Duff House Club. This was finally agreed on 1 January 1925, although the links course continued to be used until 1929.

The Duff House Club owes its origin to the famous and splendid eighteenth-century mansion built by William Adam for William Duff, the first Earl of Fife.

The sixth Earl of Fife, Alexander Duff, was born in 1849, and as a bachelor crony, it is reported, of Edward Prince of Wales (later King Edward VII) astonished and pleased the royal family by wishing to marry at the age of forty the Prince of Wales's eldest daughter Princess Louise, the Princess Royal, who was then but twenty-two years old. Queen Victoria made the Earl the first Duke of Fife, and the royal couple settled down at East Sheen in Richmond Park, at Mar Lodge at Braemar on Deeside, and at Duff House, Banff. Both the Duke and the Princess Royal were keen golfers to the extent of employing a private professional named Harris and laying out some golf-holes both at Duff House and at Mar Lodge.

In November 1906 the Duke, who was clearly a man of extraordinary generosity, gave absolutely and without restriction the Duff House estate with 140 acres of land to the twin towns of Banff and Macduff to improve their resources and attractions and provide land for golf and other recreations. This huge gift, administered by a trust set up by the two towns, over the years seemed an almost unmanageably large cuckoo in the nest, but it was the background for setting up the Duff House Golf Club in 1909 on the estuarine land close by the river Deveron which separates the two towns. An 18-hole course was laid out, with a bogey of 81 for its 5888 yards, and was formally opened by that forbidding Scots amateur Mure Fergusson, followed by exhibition games by J. H. Taylor and James Braid.

In spite of what the professionals said at the opening in 1909, the course was, it seems, deadly dull, with square greens mown from the ends of the fairways.

World War I all but killed the Duff House Club: most of the course was ploughed up for crops, and in 1919 the Club's funds were £9 0s 5½d and a year later 8d. The members held on, however; a whip-round of half-a-crown a head contributed to the Secretary's personal deficit, and the 18 holes were opened again in 1923. It was recognized, however, that these were not good enough, and, amid controversy with Macduff Town council, with Banff Town Council and within their own committee, the Club decided to go for a first-class layout – the present course, in fact, to the design of the famous Dr Alister Mackenzie, later to be the architect of the world-famous Augusta National and Cypress Point courses in America.

Meanwhile the Duchess of Fife, widowed since 1912 and no longer a local resident, watched the revival of the Duff House Golf Club with sympathy. In December 1923 a Royal Valediction was read in which she expressed the wish to become Patroness of the Club and desiring it to be known as the Duff House Royal Golf Club, her own choice of title. When the amalgamation with Banff Golf Club took place on 1 January 1925 the Duff House Royal title was adopted.

The Mackenzie course was opened in August 1924 by Sandy Herd and Ted Ray, each of whom scored 71 in just under two hours. Each of the pros said what a fine course it was – and so it is. World War II did serious harm to the club's fortunes, but once again the members held on, although the full 18 holes were not restored until 1949.

In 1961 the twin towns began to sell off part of the great estate, and Macdonald Estates of Edinburgh bought a part of it. Of this, 35 acres were rented by the Club, which was able to buy them for £3500. Later, scared by the imminent disappearance of the two town councils under the local government reorganization of 1975, the towns agreed to sell to Duff House Royal the rest of the land on which the course stood, 65 acres. A favourable deal was struck by the Club, and now Duff House Royal stands with all its own buildings on its own land on a first-class site with a good golf-course to play on.

King Edward VII, whose daughter granted a royal title to Duff House Royal and Royal Tarlair, seen with her, Princess Louise, Duchess of Fife

ROYAL TARLAIR GOLF CLUB, MACDUFF

This club has much in common with the Duff House Royal in the neighbouring town of Banff, inasmuch as the course is built on land which was once part of the estates of the Duke of Fife. According to Dr Robert Henry, the President of the club and former Provost of Macduff, the club paid a rent to the Fife estate for a feu or permanent leasehold of the land. This was in 1926, when the club was formed. At the same time it acquired its royal title from the Dowager Duchess because it occupied her ducal land. The title grant, we are told, is permanent, though no documents survive.

In the 1960s this part of the Fife Estate was sold to Macdonald Estates, who later sold it to the Burgh of Macduff for £5000, who in turn leased it to the golf club. In 1975, when the disappearance of the town councils was imminent, Macduff Council sold the 99 acres of land occupied by Royal Tarlair for £5000, plus interest on the money they had spent since buying it from Macdonald Estates. The Council then gave the Club a grant of a like amount.

Royal Tarlair is a natural cliff-top course on the outskirts of Macduff on the Moray Firth. The once famous mineral springs of Tarlair were near here, hence the name. In World War I a German mine came ashore here and blew up, destroying the spring, which has not since been found.

Although the course is of recent origin, golf, of a crude sort, was played for generations on the links down by the harbour at Macduff. While the present course is not one of the most famous or exacting in Scotland, except when the wind asserts itself, the views from the course of sea and hill as far away as Caithness are splendid. Perhaps the short 13th is the most notable hole, reminiscent of the famous 7th at Pebble Beach, with its green right on the rocky shore and a little bay to cross.

THE ROYAL BURGESS GOLFING SOCIETY OF EDINBURGH

Although, as we have seen, this is the oldest of all the golf clubs in the world, it only received the royal title very late in its history – not until 1929 in fact. In the 1920s and 1930s the then Prince of Wales, later Edward VIII, and his brother the Duke of York, later George VI, played at the Barnton course whenever they visited Edinburgh. Indeed the Duke of York liked the club and course so well that he petitioned for membership in May 1929, using the prescribed form of address to the Honourable the Captain, Council and members of the Society, humbly shewing that 'your Petitioner is an ardent admirer and Player of the ancient and manly Game of Golf and is desirous of being admitted a member of your Honourable Society', and ending: 'May it therefor please you to admit your Petitioner as a member of your Honourable Society and your Petitioner will ever play' – signed 'Albert'. Needless to say the Petitioner was admitted, and as an honorary member.

In 1928 and 1929 Sir Robert Boothby was Captain, and it was he who was mainly instrumental in gaining the royal title for the club. This was done through the Secretary of State for Scotland's office, although no letter of application exists. The Scottish Office, however, wrote on 30 September 1929 to say that the club's application had been laid before King George V, who had been 'graciously pleased to command that the Society shall hereafter be known as the Royal Burgess Golfing Society of Edinburgh'.

In 1935 the Prince of Wales accepted the captaincy of the Society, which he relinquished on becoming King in January 1936. His brother when he became King awarded the Society his Patronage. When the former King Edward VIII died as Duke of Windsor in 1972, his badge of office was returned to the club.

ROYAL TROON GOLF CLUB

This is the last of the royal golf clubs of Scotland, indeed the last of all. It is, however, the first with this distinction in the west of Scotland, all the other nine being on the eastern edge of the land.

Royal Troon by Scottish standards is a comparatively modern club, dating from 1878, since when it has played an important part in the development of the game, particularly since it came into the championship rota in 1923. It was therefore fitting that the

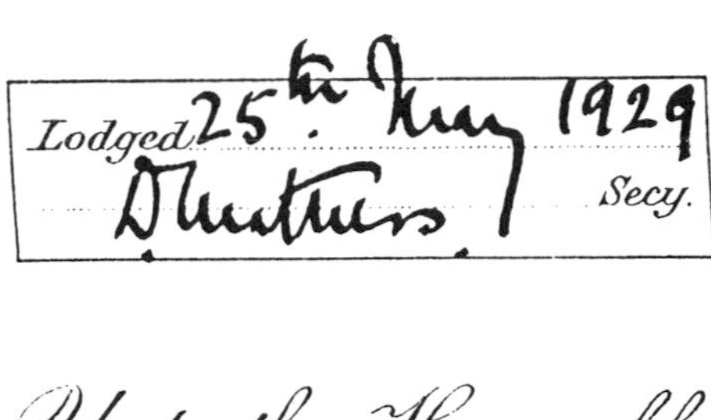

Lodged 25th May 1929
[illegible] Secy.

Admitted 27th June 1929
Captain.

Unto the Honorable the Captain, Council and Members of The Edinburgh Burgess Golfing Society.

The Petition of

Name His Royal Highness Prince Albert Frederick Arthur George

Profession or Occupation Duke of York K.G. K.T. P.C. G.C.V.O. G.C.M.G

Address 145 Piccadilly London. W1

A petition of HRH The Duke of York for membership of the Edinburgh Burgess Golfing Society

honour of the royal title should have been granted in its centenary year, 1978.

The land on which the club constructed its course lies close to the shore of the Ayrshire coast to the north of Prestwick Links, and is owned by the Duke of Portland, who became the Club's first President. In 1921 the Club bought the freehold of this land, on which by then three courses stood.

This big links has now been the host to the Open Championship five times and to the Amateur four times. The Open first came here in 1923, when Arthur Havers beat off the American menace, but it was Arnold Palmer's win in 1962 that was the most spectacular, for, although the course was exceptionally dry and many of the players couldn't cope, he spreadeagled the field. Only six rounds under 70 were recorded in the entire championship, three of them by Arnie. It was Palmer who, almost single-handed, put our Open Championship back as a major event, and he was deservedly honoured by Royal Troon in 1982 with a life membership. 'At the ceremony he was much moved and also much loved.'

Another famous victory here was that of a close friend of mine, Charlie Yates, who won the Amateur in 1938, the first time it was played at Troon. Later that year my friend

The new crest of Royal Troon, approved by the Lord Lyon, King of Arms

endeared himself to a huge audience by singing 'A Wee Duoch and Doris' from the steps of the R & A club house in St Andrews in celebration of Britain and Ireland's win in the Walker Cup.

Lest we be carried away from our review of 'Royal Golf', it is time to shut down on history and confine our description of this great links to that of the short 8th hole, the 'Postage Stamp', the shortest and one of the most respected holes in championship golf. It is 126 yards long, small of green in proportion to its length, and beset with deep and grasping bunkers. Terrible disasters have happened here – 15 was scored by a German player in the 1950 Open – but best of all was 71-year-old Gene Sarazen's hole in one here in his last championship in 1973, fifty years after his first Open (also here).

In April 1978 Major Boucher-Myers, the Captain of the Club, wrote to the Secretary of State for Scotland in Edinburgh requesting, with the support of the Scottish Golf Union, that a formal application for the royal title should be placed before the Queen. Information in support of this petition was supplied, most importantly perhaps Troon's status as a championship course and its hundred years of existence.

In a letter dated 19 May 1978, the Club received the glad news that its request had been granted, as follows:

Scottish Home and Health Department
New St Andrew's House
Edinburgh EH1 3TF
19 May 1978

Major B W S Boucher-Myers DSO
Captain, Troon Golf Club
Troon, Ayrshire

Sir

With reference to your letter of 17 April, I am directed by the Secretary of State to inform you that he has submitted to The Queen the request by the Troon Golf Club to be granted the title 'Royal', to which Her Majesty has been graciously pleased to accede and directs that the club shall be named accordingly.

I am, Sir
Your obedient Servant
(Sgd.) A T F OGILVIE

This letter drew the following gracious exchange:

Troon Golf Club
Troon, Ayrshire

The Rt. Hon. Bruce Millan M.P.
Secretary of State for Scotland,
Scottish Office,
New St Andrew's House,
Edinburgh EH1 3TF

25th May, 1978

Sir,

I wish to convey to you the very sincere thanks of all members of Troon Golf Club for having placed before The Queen the Club's request to be granted the title 'Royal'.

Please convey to Her Majesty how conscious we are of the honour she has bestowed

Right: A tournament at the Troon Golf Club in 1887

1
2
3
4
5
J. Finnemore

upon us and the pride with which we will hold our Royal title.

I have the honour to be, Sir,

Your obedient Servant,

(Sgd.) B W S BOUCHER-MYERS

Captain

Royal Troon Golf Club

Scottish Home and Health Department
New St Andrew's House
Edinburgh EH1 3TF

B W S Boucher-Myers Esq
Captain, Troon Golf Club
Troon, Ayrshire

31 May 1978

Dear Sir

With reference to your letter of 25 May, the Secretary of State is happy to convey to Her Majesty the Club's loyal message on the occasion of the grant of the title 'Royal' to mark its centenary.

This signal honour is the first to be granted to any Golf Club during Her Majesty's reign, the last such recognition being accorded by the late King George VI in 1951 to the Royal Birkdale Club.

For his part, the Secretary of State has asked me to convey his own good wishes for the Royal Troon's continuing success.

Yours faithfully

(Sgd.) A T F OGILVIE

Later in the year 1978 the Club made a petition to the Lord Lyon King of Arms for the grant of arms, perhaps more correctly 'ensigns armorial', to be used on ties, buttons, cutlery, crockery, etc.

To this the Lord Lyon replied, in the fine wording of Herald's College, that:

> We have Devised and Do by these Presents Assign, Ratify and Confirm unto the Petitioners for and on behalf of the Royal Troon Golf Club with such due and congruent differences as may hereafter be severally matriculated for them, the following Ensigns Armorial as depicted on the margin hereof [not shown] and matriculated of even date with These Presents upon the—page of the—volume of Our Public Register of All Arms and Bearings in Scotland, videlicet:
> *Azure edged Or, five ancient golf clubs, one poleways and two on either side in Saltire Argent all bound together by a thong in the likeness and shape of a coiled serpent of the Second, the whole surmounted by a ducal coronet of the last, in chief two crosses moline of the Third*, and in an Escrol below the same this Motto 'TAM ARTE QUAM MARTE' by demonstration of which Ensigns Armorial he and his successors in the same are amongst all Nobles and in all Places of Honour, to be taken, numbered, accounted and received as an Incorporated Noble in the Noblesse of Scotland . . .

To all of this one can only say that here are honours well earned, the only royal golf title in the last thirty-six years and the only one granted by Queen Elizabeth II.

CHAPTER 4

Royal Household golf

As we have seen, King Edward VII enjoyed mild golf and had a course laid out at Windsor, as Sir Frederick Ponsonby in *Recollections of Three Reigns** describes:

> As golf proved so popular, the King gave orders that a golf course should be made at Windsor and wished it to be eighteen holes, but as we always took one and a half hours to do nine holes, I persuaded him to limit it to nine holes. I asked Mr Mure Fergusson, a distinguished amateur player who had laid out a course called New Zealand at Woking, to come down and sketch out the Windsor Castle links. He came down and took infinite trouble. We had men with stakes to mark the right and left of each bunker, and a man with a tape measure. Mure Fergusson succeeded in laying out nine good holes ending up just below the East Terrace, and I gave instructions to the farm bailiff to have the bunkers made.
>
> I did not go to Windsor for two months as I presumed that a competent firm had been employed, but I suddenly received an irate telegram from the King to the effect that the private Park at Windsor had been ruined and that I was to order the bunkers to be rased to the ground. When I went to Windsor I was aghast at what I saw. The man who had undertaken to make the bunkers had obviously no knowledge of golf grounds and didn't know the ABC of the business. At each post which had been driven into the ground to make the right and left of the bunkers he had erected a mound four feet high and a ditch four feet deep but only ten yards long. The result was that the ground looked like a graveyard with tombstones dotted about. I was furious and went in search of the man. I found him talking to the farm bailiff. He said that he proposed to make the last bunker in the shape of a Victoria Cross with flowers! I told him what I thought of him and said it was criminal of him to undertake a job like this when he had not the most elementary knowledge of bunkers. I gave orders that he and his men were to

ROYAL HOUSEHOLD GOLF CLUB

WINDSOR

*Sir Frederick Ponsonby, *Recollections of Three Reigns* (London: Quartet, 1988).

leave the ground at once, and I told the farm bailiff to see that they never returned. We had a breezy five minutes, and I closed the discussion by saying that unless he and his men cleared out in an hour I would instruct the police to push them out. I gave orders that the bunkers were to be rased to the ground, and sent for the professional from the Datchet links close by and explained to him how the bunkers should go, asking him to superintend the work. Eventually this came out all right and Mure Fergusson came down and made a few alterations. He was a big red-faced man and probably accustomed to have his way, but when the King happened to come along he became tongue-tied. It was unfortunate that I did not have an opportunity of explaining what a swell he was in the golfing world because the King thought he was a professional. However, when I explained everything afterwards to the King he sent him a cigarette-case with the Royal cypher on it.

Other leading golfers were invited to play with the King. First of all Kirkaldy came down from Scotland, but he got rather drunk and was sent back. Then Ben Sayers came and was a great success. He was always anxious to praise the King's shots and once when the King topped his drive, he exclaimed 'Very good direction, Your Majesty'. Once when the King said he would play at three o'clock Sayers teed up two new balls ready but received a message that the King would not play till four, so he went away. Meanwhile Queen Alexandra came out to play and, finding two new balls, played a sort of hockey with them till they were battered into a three-cornered shape. She then replaced the balls on the tee and went in. At four the King came out and asked Sayers if he had got any golf balls. He replied that they were ready on the tee, but when the King saw them he thought Sayers was trying to be funny. Luckily Sayers had plenty more, but it was not till tea-time that the King learnt that the Queen and Princess Victoria had played golf at three, and grasped why the balls were so battered.

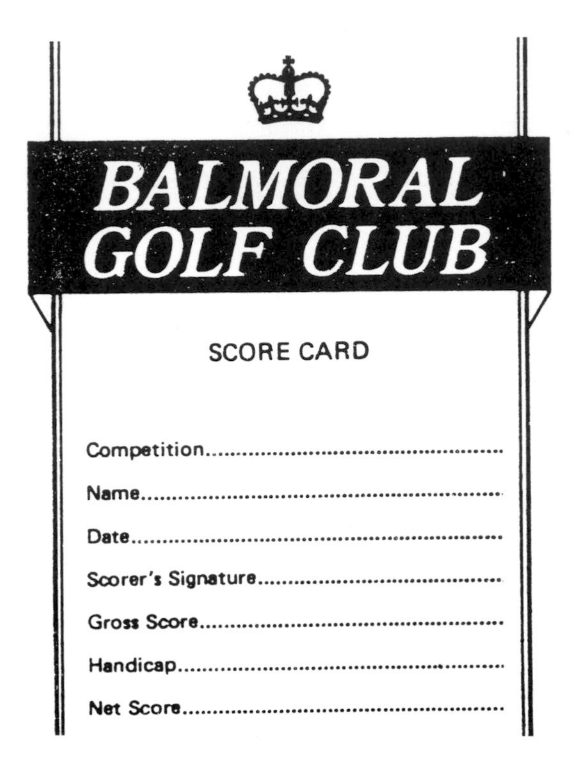
BALMORAL GOLF CLUB

SCORE CARD

Competition....................

Name....................

Date....................

Scorer's Signature....................

Gross Score....................

Handicap....................

Net Score....................

This course in Windsor Park still remains for members of the Royal Household and staff to play on, and, as Mr Audis, the Secretary of the Royal Burgess Society, said, with the 9 holes at Balmoral must make the longest course in the world.

I had hoped to be able to make a visit here and perhaps obtain a photograph of one of the greens, with the Castle towering up behind, as the course is spectacularly placed under the eastern flank of the hill on which Windsor Castle stands. Unfortunately, the Comptroller of the Lord Chamberlain's Office had to refuse my request, as the course, unlike that of Balmoral, lies within a security area. He did, however, send me an attractive card of the course which is worth reproducing. It shows that the play of the 9 holes can be varied by the use of alternative tees, as there are two at each hole, and that the card rather unusually starts at the 16th hole, which is the one nearest the Castle, rather than at the 1st, which is further out.

The Balmoral course, which we were able

to have a look at in July 1987, is a pleasant 9-hole park course with some attractive hill shots and slopes and hollows with fine trees. It is by no means a 'straight-up-and-down the field' layout. The course and greens are well kept and measure 2235 yards with a par of 33; there are four short holes, ranging from 96 to 233 yards, and one par-5. There are two tees at each hole to add variety to the round.

This course is kept for the benefit of the staff and household at Balmoral, with friends by invitation.

Another Royal Household golf course, which we cannot class as a true royal *club*, was laid out on the estate of the Duke and Duchess of Fife at Mar Lodge, Braemar, on Deeside. As we have seen, the Duke and his consort, the Princess Royal, were keen golfers and did much to support golf at Banff. Harris, their private professional, with the aid of the Factor, laid out a 9-hole course at Mar Lodge in 1909 for the use of the tenantry and employees of the Mar estates and their friends in the vicinity. The club was launched with due ceremony under the name of the Royal Craggan Golf Club, with some sixty members. The Princess Royal gave a cup for competition and the two Princesses, Alexandra and Maud, gave medals.

We made enquiries at the neighbouring Braemar Golf Club, which occupies a beautiful setting along the river Clunie amid the Grampian mountains, one of which, Beinn A'Bhuird, still carried snow in mid-July. Here we heard that Royal Craggan had been abandoned in 1939 when war broke out, and later the estate was sold. One of its members, Mr Fred Maclaren, who was an estate worker, rescued the Princess Royal's cup and gave it to the Braemar Club, who compete for it regularly as the Craggan Cup.

Created by the inspiration and drive of the great J. H. Taylor, of whom we shall hear more later two public courses were created on the Crown Lands of Windsor Park: the Prince's Course, opened in 1922 by the Prince of Wales, later King Edward VIII; and the Duke's Course, opened in 1925 by the Duke of York, later King George VI.

CHAPTER 5

Over the Border – the pioneers

Golf came to life in England just about a century later than in Scotland and in much the same way. Groups of congenial friends, often expatriate Scots or egged on by Scotsmen, got together to form clubs and societies, playing on common land or open heath. Westward Ho! and the public common land of Braunton Burrows, Hoylake and the old Wirral race-course, Wimbledon Common, Tooting Bec and Mitcham Common, with a very early bird in Manchester in 1818 on Kersal Moor, are all names we associate with this period. Old Manchester disappears from these pages as it never became royal. It does seem to have lost its way rather, although that mine of information *The Golfer's Handbook* records it as surviving with sixty members 'temporarily without a course'.

But one name stands out ahead of all these others and stands out quite alone as the pioneer of English Golf, and that is Royal Blackheath.

ROYAL BLACKHEATH

This is without question the premier club in Britain outside Scotland, indeed in the world. It is a strongly held tradition in the club that a Society of Blackheath Golfers was formed in 1608 by the Scots who came south in considerable numbers when the thrones were united in 1603 under James I. There is no reason to doubt that golf was played on Blackheath about this time or even earlier. There was a royal palace here, and as James I and his sons Henry and Charles were keen golfers we can be sure that they played golf when in residence. Charlton House, Blackheath, was built for Prince Henry, and Sir Adam Newton, whom the Prince nearly struck with his golf-club, lived here. The difficulty is to establish the date of formation of the *club*. Records were destroyed in a fire at the end of the eighteenth century, or perhaps deliberately 'lost' to preserve some Masonic secrets, and the earliest fact that can be established is that on 16 August 1766 a silver club was presented to 'the Honourable Company of Goffers at Blackheath', while written records start with a list of subscribers of 'The Goff Club at the Chocolate House at Blackheath' for 1787. This list shows almost all the members to be Scots, though the Treasurer bore the sound Sassenach name of Kensington.

Golf on the stony common land of Blackheath survived in the old primitive form until after World War I. Originally, there were 5 holes which avoided the old gravel pits on the heath, but from 1844 a new layout of 7 holes which traversed the gravel pits was made. These gravel pits played a part in the history of London. They had been dug first to provide stone for the rebuilding of London after the Great Fire in 1666. They were largely filled in with the rubble produced by the Blitz of 1940–41.

The new holes, bearing in mind the powers of the feathery and later the gutty ball, must have been a sore trial, for they measured 170, 335, 380, 540, 500, 230 and 410 yards to a total of 2565 yards. It is small wonder that

Above: *A golf match at Blackheath in 1870 and* (below) *Medal Day at Blackheath*

the course record made by Mr A. S. Johnston in 1910 with a rubber-cored ball was 95, or eleven over-4s for 21 holes, at a time when most 18-hole course records were below 70.

The best professionals of the day, J. H. Taylor, James Braid and Harry and Tom Vardon, played a medal competition over 21 holes at Blackheath in July 1908 to commemorate the 300th anniversary of the date on which the Club was 'instituted' and the 50th anniversary of the Club's victory in the first open tournament held at St Andrews in 1857. JH won the prize with a score of 96 – equivalent to 82 for 18 holes. Braid and Tom Vardon took 97, and brother Harry scored 99. In the afternoon, in a fourball, Tom Vardon did one round in 28, a remarkable score.

Bernard Darwin in *Green Memories*, his delightful autobiography published in 1928, wrote:

> Hordes of football players have driven the golfers at last from their historic heath and they play now at Eltham. I am glad to remember that on my last visit to the Club I had a putting match with the Field-Marshal on the home green, the hole having in accordance with immemorial custom no tin in it, and was well beaten by his wooden putter.

A personal check made sixty years later found that the last hole at Eltham now had its regulation tin.

In 1923, when golf had become impossible on the open heath, the Club amalgamated with the Eltham Golf Club and withdrew to its present site on Crown land in Eltham Park. Here the Club, with its incomparable collection of trophies, pictures and china, is suitably housed in Eltham Lodge, a superb seventeenth-century house built in 1664 by Hugh May for Sir John Shaw, banker to King Charles II. This gives a proper atmosphere, which so important and historic a club should have, for the course, a good parkland circuit with fine trees and a lake, laid out by James Braid and subsequently modified by Frank Pennink in 1970, cannot with the best will in the world provide it.

It is for this reason that attention and interest are inevitably aroused more inside than outside the club house. It is no surprise that the course and club house were considerably knocked about during World War II, the worst damage being from a delayed-action parachute-mine, from the blast of which, it was said by Paddy Connolly, the steward who was present, 'the whole club house rose up about 1½ inches and fell back'.

The Club's trophies are a splendid array, including the Spring Medal, originally the gold medal of the Knuckle Club (the old Blackheath Winter Club), which dates back to 1792, the silver club of 1766 and the newer ones to accommodate the silver balls affixed by the captains after the old one was full. There is also a fine collection of eighteenth-century china, including punch bowls and four joram jugs, which hold about a gallon, used no doubt for claret to pay the fines, forfeits or bets of the members.

The pictures are attractive, including the almost lifesize portrait by Lemuel Francis Abbot of Henry Callender in red coat, white knee breeches and silk stockings, which is found in reproductions in many parts of the world. He was Captain in 1790, 1801 and 1807.

The most famous of all golfing pictures, that of William Innes, Captain in 1778, painted by Abbot in 1790, is lost; if it turned up one day – and stranger things have happened – what a find that would be for the Club. Meanwhile, like thousands of golf clubs all over the world, Royal Blackheath has to be content with a print. Who hasn't seen it: Innes with a proud look, in the uniform of a past captain – red coat, white breeches and silk hose, buckle shoes and a fine big black hat worn at a jaunty angle – with a club over his shoulder? Behind is his 'college man' or caddie in a tricorn hat with a bundle of clubs under his arm and a bottle in his pocket, wearing the dress of a pensioner of the Royal Naval Hospital at Greenwich; in the background is a windmill. One theory is that the picture still exists immured in a private collection in Fife; another belief is that it was destroyed in the Indian Mutiny. The naval pensioners were of value to the Club, providing caddies, fore-caddies and green-keepers on competition days. It was a sad day when the Hospital closed in 1869.

Most appealing are the paintings of Old Alick, born in 1756, who served under Nelson at Trafalgar. Alick Brotherson was a caddie until it was minuted in October 1833 that 'it was proposed and carried that poor old Alick's allowance be increased to 2s 6d per week and that he be restrained from carrying clubs and confine himself to taking care of the holes'. Here is the dear old man in breeches and a top hat carrying two iron clubs, with windmills and players in the background.

A recent addition to Blackheath's pictures is a delightful water-colour by C. E. Cundell of Corporal Sharpe, the club-maker, painted in 1833. The Club also has a notable museum of old golf-clubs and golf-balls. It is a joy to be able to look on the very club that Henry Callender is holding in his famous picture.

The most celebrated player at Blackheath was George Glennie from St Andrews, who was Captain in 1862–4 and Hon. Secretary from 1868 to 1886. Glennie, who presented a medal to the Club, which in turn presented a replica to the R & A, held the amateur record at St Andrews from 1855 to 1879 with a score of 88. Glennie and Lt J. C. Stewart of the 72nd Highlanders, as we have seen, won the first golf championship ever played, at St Andrews.

Blackheath was conspicuous in giving a helping hand to new clubs starting up, including Royal Calcutta in 1830, Royal North Devon at Westward Ho! and Royal Liverpool at Hoylake in the 1860s.

Blackheath's royal title provokes some uncertainty. We read in the Club's excellent publication of 1981 that Edward Prince of Wales agreed to become Patron in 1899 and when he became King in 1901 continued his patronage and granted the royal title. However, earlier records show that the Club was already known as 'Royal Blackheath', notably in the illuminated scroll of the Great Tournament, describing the Club's victory in 1857. It seems unlikely that in those more formal days the Club could possibly have allowed itself to be called 'Royal' without some clear entitlement.

ROYAL NORTH DEVON, WESTWARD HO!

Here is historic turf indeed, the first English golf links and the first outside Scotland, at Westward Ho! named after Charles Kingsley's famous novel, which was written here. Golf was started here in a primitive way in 1853 by the family of the vicar of Northam, the Rev. I. H. Gosset. In 1860 old Tom Morris was brought down from Prestwick, where he was then stationed, to advise, and in 1864 the Club was formed, with the vicar the first captain, as the North Devon and West of England Golf Club. It remains the oldest club in England playing on its original land.

Tom Morris came down again in 1864, and made two layouts, one of 17 and the other of 22 holes. The links, which has been altered several times since, lies on some low land called the Burrows, under the wing of the great Pebble Ridge, which protects it from the sea, and Barnstaple Bay. Sandhills march with the Pebble Ridge and come into play in the first half. General Moncrieff, of St Andrews, on coming here to stay with the vicar in about 1860, said: 'Providence evidently designed this for a golf course.'

Westward Ho!, like Brancaster or Ballybunion, remains a supreme example of natural seaside golf, and it hasn't been altered since Herbert Fowler's reconstruction in 1908; in spite of that, its difficulties are almost as great as in the days of the founders, like Captain Molesworth, 'Old Mole', and

Ladies' Day at Westward Ho! in 1873

his three sons. The links is on common land and the commoners can and do graze horses, sheep and cattle on the Burrows, sometimes as many as 1000 sheep and 100 horses and ponies. These have at times rather soiled the course. The unique characteristic of Westward Ho! is the rushes which form the rough at many of the inland holes; up to shoulder-height and 'as thick as a hedge', they end in iron-tipped spikes which can impale you with ridiculous ease, or spear a ball from cover to cover. You have to play over them or play along them and pray that you won't get in them.

The Club's 100th anniversary book tells us: 'In 1867, chiefly owing to the energy and keenness of the Rev. Lymebear Harding, the Hon. Secretary, His Royal Highness the Prince of Wales graciously consented to give his patronage to the Club, the title of which became the Royal North Devon and West of England Golf club.'

The Amateur Championship has been here three times, first in 1912, when John Ball won for the eighth and last time, beating Abe Mitchell, at the 38th hole; then again in 1925, when Robert Harris won; and for the last time in 1931, when a surprise winner – and none more surprised than he – was Eric Martin Smith, just down from Cambridge. But for its remoteness, there is no doubt that more use would have been made of this great course.

Some very great golfers were nurtured on

this links: Horace Hutchinson, the graceful and gifted amateur, who twice won the Amateur Championship, and John Henry Taylor, five times Open Champion, who died here in his ninety-third year. And what a splendid character he was, forthright, vehement and brave. JH was fond of the Johnsonian 'sir' and used to say things thrice for emphasis. In his shop in Mid-Surrey was a picture of W. G. Grace, for once not attired for cricket; so I asked JH what sort of a game the Doctor played, and he said: 'Like a boy, sir; like a boy, sir; like a boy.' I remember also his answer when we were watching the University Match at Prince's, in which his son Jack was playing, to a question I had put to him. One of the Cambridge men seemed to be frittering away a lead and I asked JH: 'Do you think he'll crack?' 'Crack, crack, he hasn't the brains to crack.'

Apart from his distinction as a great golfer in the immortal Triumvirate, JH did much to raise the status of the professional, which in his early days was little above that of caddie and often miserably paid. When he retired, the profession was everywhere respected and was on the threshold of the million-dollar business golf has now become. The extent to which the great Triumvirate dominated British golf is perhaps forgotten today. Suffice it to say that between them they won sixteen of the twenty-one Open Championships from 1894 to 1914, six going to Harry Vardon and five each to J. H. Taylor and James Braid. JH could also be a speaker of rare charm, and I will always remember his speech after the University Match dinner at Sandwich in 1928, when he thanked all present with a sincerity and emotion, which none could doubt, for being kind to his son, but in a way which showed that he had learned 'to distinguish between sentiment and sentimentality', so that no one was embarrassed, neither his son nor his son's friends. JH always said that his son's election to the presidency of the Junior Common Room at his college pleased him more than any championship he ever won.

In another way, surely 'Old Mole', another Westward Ho! character, must have been a great figure: always ready for a bet and a sharp match with one of his sons as partner. He lived to a ripe old age, until he was almost ninety in fact. On 5 September 1877, he set out to test the wager he'd made at Whitsun to walk the 3 miles to the links, play six rounds under 660 strokes carrying his own clubs, and walk home before dark. He started at 6.10 a.m. and had a bad round of 120, followed by 105 and 122. The next three rounds were 108, 102 and 105, to a total of 662 for six rounds. Not put out by this, 'Old Mole' played a seventh round of 114 to make his total inside 660 by discarding the first round. On top of this, he was home by twenty minutes to seven. There was great argument over this result – some said the first six rounds constituted the bet, others that the seventh round was admissible. Who won the bet? History doesn't record, but I'd find for the Captain.

Another golfer of great promise was Johnny Bramston, who died young, and at the other end of the scale Westward Ho! produced the oldest winner of the Amateur Championship, the Hon. Michael Scott, who won at Hoylake in 1937 at the age of fifty-five.

Frank Pennink writes: 'Westward Ho! is a historic club in historic surroundings; it is worth every trouble, or any length of journey, to play golf there.'

Few people, indeed, have chewed up the course here. In the first hundred years of the Club's history, only four scores under 70 were registered in the Club's medal competitions. In another competition R. C. Champion had a 65, a phenomenal score, but otherwise the honours boards until the last decade show almost as many scores in the 80s as in the 70s. After all, there are 102 bunkers on the course, and there used to be more, not to mention the rushes.

Let Bernard Darwin have the last word: 'If

you have done anything near eighty, you may be thoroughly pleased with yourself, unless you are a very eminent person indeed', and this: 'Without entering into invidious comparisons there is, for the fun and adventure of the game, no more ideal piece of golfing country in the world.'

I should say in closing that in this account I have drawn liberally on my previous writing on Westward Ho! in *Play the Best Courses*.

ROYAL WIMBLEDON GOLF CLUB

Close on the heels of the start of the golf club at Westward Ho! came the formation of a club by members of the London Scottish Rifle Volunteers in November 1864.

Wimbledon Common, which provided a shooting-range for the volunteers, was its home, and the whole matter was put on a proper military footing by an order issued by the Commanding Officer of the London Scottish, Lord Elcho, in May 1866.

A 7-hole course was laid out on the Common with the permission of the Lord of the Manor, whose rights were later transferred to a Board of Conservators elected by the local ratepayers. By 1871 the course was extended to 18 holes, laid out by Tom Dunn. A room in the local headquarters building of the LSRV, the Iron House, was reserved for the golfers and the members and honorary members of the regiment.

By 1869, members from other branches of the armed services, other clubs and local residents were admitted, a privilege soon extended to all comers. By the early 1870s the non-military members much outnumbered the soldiery, but the all-powerful Elcho retained control. Friction developed, and a long wrangle between the regimental bosses and the more numerous civilian members ended with the Club splitting into two separate clubs in 1882: the London Scottish Golf Club and the Wimbledon Golf Club, with premises at either end of this rather hard, uncompromising stony heath.

At the time of the separation Colonel Moncrieff, on behalf of the Wimbledon Golf Club, petitioned the Prince of Wales (later Edward VII) to continue as Patron of the Club under its new name and grant the title of 'Royal'. The Prince replied that he would be pleased to be Patron but that he had not the power to grant the title, which had to be negotiated through the Home Office. That was done, and on 6 June 1882 the Queen graciously granted the title to the Royal Wimbledon Golf Club.

In 1907 Royal Wimbledon moved to private grounds nearby with a course laid out at Caesar's Camp by Willie Park. This course took some time to develop, and members of the Club continued to play on the Common course until 1915. Later their place was filled by the Common Club, who use it to this day and wear red coats to warn other users of the Common that a dangerous game is afoot.

In 1924 a redesigned course to the layout of H. S. Colt was opened, and this is the fine course that Royal Wimbledon uses today. Considering that the course is only 8 miles from Hyde Park Corner, it has an atmosphere of extraordinary seclusion, and its heather, gorse and birch trees are a pleasing surprise.

The first Oxford v Cambridge University Golf Match was played on Wimbledon Common in 1878 and won by Oxford. In all, sixteen of these university matches were played here.

The Prince of Wales (later Edward VIII) was Captain of Royal Wimbledon in 1928–9 and President from 1931 to 1935. As the able historian of the club, Mr Charles Cruikshank, tells us:

> Pride of place in the deception stakes must go to the five caddies guilty of the ultimate crime in golf – although it may be argued in their defence that as loyal subjects they gave great pleasure to their heir to the throne. The conspiracy – to allow the Prince of Wales in his

Right: Golfing at Royal Wimbledon in 1888

PUTTING
A VETERAN
BY THE WINDMILL
"FORE" ! A LONG BALL
IN A BUNKER
IN AMONGST THE HAZARDS

year as Captain to believe that he had done a hole in one – had to be carefully planned. It was necessary to find a hole which His Royal Highness (handicap 12) could credibly reach from the tee in one shot, where the green could not be seen from the tee, and where the accomplice of the four caddying for the royal party could be concealed and yet see the drives – the last being essential if the Prince's ball was to be identified.

The Sixth hole at Royal Wimbledon happily meets all these criteria. It is just within reach of a 12 handicap golfer, it is masked from the tee by the majestic sweep of the rampart of Caesar's Camp, and there is ample cover in the vicinity of the green. All the fifth caddy had to do was to wait for a day when the Prince's tee shot carried over the rampart to disappear from the royal driver's view, collect the ball, drop it in the hole, and, mission accomplished, make his escape. The plan worked perfectly. The royal party was overjoyed. The caddies received record tips, which had to be abated by one fifth to provide for their accomplice. The Evening News devoted headlines to the notable event.

THE ROYAL LIVERPOOL GOLF CLUB, HOYLAKE

This is the pre-eminent English golf club, fit to be classed with the Royal and Ancient, the Honourable Company or the Edinburgh Burgesses. The Club is royal by name and royal by reputation. As Bernard Darwin wrote, 'it belongs to the whole world of golf, for it has played a great part in the history of the game'.

Here in 1885 the Amateur Championship was inaugurated; here in 1921 the amateur men of Britain met the amateur men of the United States for the first time. Here in 1902 the men of England first played the men of Scotland, and here in 1925 the local player Froes Ellison won the first English Amateur Championship.

The Amateur Championship has been played sixteen times at Hoylake and the Open ten times, and every other tournament of importance has been held here. In 1902 both the Open and the Amateur Championships were at Hoylake, and both were won by players using the new and controversial rubber-cored ball, at which point the controversy ended. Here in 1907, the happy and gifted Frenchman Arnaud Massy was the first foreigner to win our Open Championship, and here in 1930 the incomparable Bobby Jones, in my view the greatest player of all time, won the second of his four Grand Slam championships. Alas, because of the demand for space for car parks and for the huge commercial fair that the Open Championship has become with its Tented Village, 1967 looks like being Hoylake's last Open, but it ended nobly when the much beloved Roberto de Vicenzo belted a great spoon-shot over the out-of-bounds cop to the heart of the 16th green, to clinch the title: at 44 its oldest winner.

Hoylake too, like all great courses, has produced its own great players. Britain's two finest amateurs, John Ball (eight times Amateur Champion and once winner of the Open) and Harold Hilton (four times Amateur Champion, once winner of the US Amateur and twice Open Champion).

And yet I suppose there is no famous links which offers less encouragement to the first glance of the visitor than Hoylake, except perhaps the Old Course of St Andrews. The view from the smoking-room at the Royal Liverpool Golf Club on the first floor of that large Victorian club house shows a wide flat space, apparently without character or guile, bounded by some uninspired examples of later Victorian and Edwardian domestic architecture to the west; it is no longer relieved by that four-square Georgian barracks built in 1792, the Royal Hotel, once owned by John Ball's father, now that it has been destroyed. Only far away on the horizon to the south and south-west is a distant range of sandhills to remind you that this is a links after all. Far away beyond, on clear days you see the hills of Wales.

Don't be put off: the reality is greatly different. First of all this is a long, tough, supremely competent golf-course, one of the toughest and most searching of the great links. You don't get away with anything; what's more, the great long pros don't make a fool of it either.

What does this rather dull field, with incongruous knee-high banks of turf called 'cops', really do to you? First of all these knee-high banks define out-of-bounds. The severe out-of-bounds between the first fairway and the practice ground, seemingly almost a right-angle dog-leg, is an example. Jamie Anderson once put five balls out of bounds at this 1st hole, in trying to avoid the rabbit warren, and exclaimed at last, 'Ma God! It's like playing up a spout!', as *Green Memories* by Bernard Darwin tells us. In spite of some criticism, these man-made difficulties at Hoylake are still in force also at the 7th and 16th.

There is also length at Hoylake and plenty of it, 7000 yards for the Open; plenty of bunkers too, though fewer than there were sixty years ago. The greens are beautiful and the fairways less uneven than on most links; the rough, on the other hand, with dwarf rose and low-growing blackberry in places, is formidable. The fairways are often narrow and require the drive to be exactly placed or else the hole remains inexorably difficult. At Hoylake, if you put your drive in the right place, the green, while not quite welcoming the second shot, does not seem unbearably hostile, as it does to a misplaced drive. It is the rewards for excellence and the penalties for incompetence which make, this such a great and such a just links, the Final Honour School, together with Muirfield perhaps, of British golf, where luck enters into it to the minimum and justice is not only done but manifestly seen to be done.

The Royal Liverpool Club has not been afraid of change, and alterations have been made several times at Hoylake since golf started there in 1869. After World War I, H. S. Colt was brought in to make momentous changes, a new green at the 8th and entirely new holes at the 11th, 12th and 13th and playing them today it's a wonder that these excellent holes were ever criticized and disliked.

After World War II many bunkers were got rid of, no doubt to reduce maintenance, for assuredly these changes didn't make the golf any easier. In time for the championship of 1967 the 3rd hole was considerably altered and made better and more elegant, while the new, short 4th is a great improvement on its dull, flat predecessor.

Patric Dickinson, who writes such good descriptive essays on golf courses, called Hoylake 'this gloomy, marvellous links, a tough epic links'. I think we can leave it by saying that if you can play to your handicap at Hoylake, Walton Heath and Newcastle's County Down, there is no course in the world that you need be afraid of.

As John Brocklehurst tells us in the Club's excellent booklet of 1986, Hoylake in 1869 was a small fishing-village with a race-course on the Warren where the Liverpool Hunt Club had held meetings since 1849. The main feature was the great four-square Royal Hotel, dating from 1792, where people came for the newly fashionable sea-bathing.

On 15 May 1869 twenty-one local gentlemen met at the Royal Hotel and resolved to form a golf club to play on the Warren and share the space with the race-course and the rabbits. A room was reserved at the hotel, 9 holes were laid out, and a young pro from St Andrews, Jack Morris, nephew of Old Tom, was engaged and remained to serve the Club for sixty years.

The original course was laid out by Robert Chambers of Edinburgh and George Morris, Old Tom's brother, starting from the hotel. Two years later, in 1871, the course was extended to 18 holes, and in 1895 came the big change when the Club left its rooms in the Royal and moved across to the splendid new club house where one is made so welcome today.

The Liverpool Golf Club's royal title came about as recorded in the minutes:

> At a meeting of the Council of the Royal Liverpool Golf Club held at the Saddle Hotel Liverpool in July 1871. Present Messrs Dowie (Chair), Milligan, Stevens, Buckle & Tweedie. Mr Tweedie intimated that in the absence of the Secretary, he had been corresponding with the Captain of the Club, Col. E. H. Kennard, in reference to obtaining one of the Royal Family as Patron of the Club, the gratifying result being that he had now the pleasure to read the following letter from Col. Elphinstone, Prince Arthur's adviser:
>
> Buckingham Palace
> 29th June 1871
>
> Mr dear Colonel Kennard,
>
> Prince Arthur* desires me to say that he will have great pleasure in accepting the Honorary Presidency of the Liverpool Golf Club.
>
> I regret that so long a delay has occurred in settling this matter but, as my previous note stated, there were unavoidable circumstances.
>
> I beg to remain
> Yours faithfully
> (Signed) H. Elphinstone
>
> So that now and henceforth the club designates itself 'The Royal Liverpool Golf Club'. The meeting expressed its gratification at this happy result and requested Mr Tweedie to acknowledge Col. Kennard's note and convey to him the best thanks of the Council for his services.

In 1901, on the death of Queen Victoria, Col. Kennard, then a past Captain, wrote to the Secretary of State at the Home Office to see if the Club was still entitled to call itself 'Royal'.

On 27 September the Under Secretary, Mr Henry Cunningham, replied in these terms:

> I am directed by Mr Secretary Ritchie to acquaint you that he has had the honour to submit to the King for His Majesty's consideration the application of the Council of the Royal Liverpool Golf Club for permission to continue the use of the prefix 'Royal' adopted in the year 1871 and that His Majesty has been graciously pleased to comply with the request and command that the club shall be called the Royal Liverpool Golf Club.

As Mr J. R. Davidson, the Secretary of the Club today, says in his letter sending, most helpfully, photocopies of the original documents, 'so we are legitimate'.

---

* Later Duke of Connaught.

CHAPTER 6

East Anglian royal clubs

It is surprising to find no fewer than five royal golf clubs in East Anglia when, for example, there are none in Yorkshire. Perhaps the explanation may be that the Prince of Wales, later Edward VII, was often at Sandringham and knew many of the East Anglian players. He certainly was a supporter of the game.

The clubs involved are these, in order of date of foundation:

1	Royal Cromer	1888
2	Royal Epping Forest	1888
3	Royal West Norfolk	1892
4	Royal Worlington and Newmarket	1893
5	Royal Norwich	1893

ROYAL CROMER GOLF CLUB

Formed in 1888, the Royal Cromer Golf Club has produced for its centenary a notable historical survey, admirably supported by photographs, on which I have unashamedly drawn.

The course from the start has occupied tracts of cliff-top downland to the east of the town of Cromer, shifting its ground from time to time to allow for expansion of the course or to replace ground lost by horrendous landslides into the sea of the unstable cliffs. Today we have a green, hilly course with gorse and scrub as rough and a few trees. It is blessed with two features: first that most decorative of utilitarian structures, a lighthouse, and secondly a view back over the town of Cromer and its shore dominated by the magnificent church tower, the tallest in Norfolk.

The Club owes much in its origins and early days of difficulty to the Harbord family, led by successive Lords Suffield. At the time of the formation of the Club in 1888, thanks to the efforts of Henry Broadhurst MP, Lord Suffield became the Club's first President. As he was a friend and sometimes host to the Prince of Wales, later Edward VII, HRH was asked and agreed to become the Club's first Patron and grant the royal title. This he did on Christmas Day 1887, eight days before the official opening of the Club on 2 January 1888, a unique distinction.

After the death of Edward VII in May 1910, the new King in due course consented to become Patron. However, in 1936 Ed-

A portrait of King Edward VII hangs in the club house at Royal Cromer

The United States ladies who played in the first international match, which later became the Curtis Cup, at Royal Cromer in 1905: Harriot Curtis (back right) and her sister Margaret (extreme right)

ward VIII declined the post, and so did his younger brother, King George VI. At that point the Home Secretary, Sir Samuel Hoare, who had long been a member at Royal Cromer, took pains to tell the Club that it could still style itself 'Royal': a title once granted continued automatically.

The greatest claim to fame for Royal Cromer is without doubt its organization of the first international golf match ever played – that of the ladies of Great Britain against America as a preliminary to the British Ladies' Championship in 1905. Matches between the ladies of England, Scotland and Ireland had been played before, but this was the first outside national boundaries. The results were:

Miss Lottie Dod (English Champion)	lost to	Miss Georgianna Bishop (American Champion)
Miss May Hezlet	beat	Miss Margaret Curtis
Miss Mary Graham	beat	Miss Molly Adams
Miss Elinor Nevile	beat	Miss Harriot Curtis
Miss Florence Hezlet	beat	Miss Emily Lockwood
Miss Alexa Glover	beat	Miss Frances Griscom
Miss Dorothy Campbell	beat	Mrs G. M. Martin
Great Britain 6 matches		US 1 match

In modern times the United States and Great Britain & Ireland ladies, after playing at Royal St George's in 1988, came to Royal Cromer, where the home team won, to celebrate the Club's centenary attired in Edwardian dress

Four members of the British team which won 6–1: Lottie Dod, Dorothy Campbell, May Hezlet and Mary Graham

As a result of this match the Curtis sisters presented the now famous Curtis Cup, which is regularly played for between the ladies of the USA and the British Isles, a contest in which our team in the USA in 1986 was the first to win against any American golf side over there. In 1988 the two Curtis Cup teams played a match at Cromer in period dress.

ROYAL EPPING FOREST GOLF CLUB

Royal Epping Forest follows the unusual pattern for England of being a private members' club using an adjoining public golf course, like some of the clubs in Scotland.

Nineteen enthusiasts decided to form a golf club in 1888 at Chingford, 11 miles as the crow flies from the centre of London, and J. G. Gibson, Captain of the Royal Blackheath, with two other golfers and two caddies, came over and laid out 9 holes of golf in Epping Forest, using as base the Royal Forest Hotel.

The management and subsequently the ownership of Epping Forest, a small residue of what was once a huge royal hunting preserve, came to the Corporation of London as 'Conservators of the Forest in lieu of the Crown' in 1878. They have maintained and cherished it for the free access and benefit of the public ever since.

Today the Corporation of London maintains the golf course and lets the REFGC play, with special privileges for its members, in return for an annual capitation fee per member. The Corporation also maintains its own club house for public use and hires the services of a professional.

The course, an unsophisticated layout, runs through the beautiful unspoilt woodlands of Epping Forest, an attractive piece of old English countryside with hardwoods – fine oaks, beech and birch, hornbeams and hollies, with not a pine in sight – predominating.

These woods are historic country beyond doubt, yet so close in to the paved streets and sodium lamps, electric railways and entry in the London telephone directory. Here it is believed Queen Boadicea made her last stand against the Romans in AD 61. Dick Turpin, it is said, killed a forest-keeper here in 1737.

Early in the Club's history, in October 1888, the Duke of Connaught agreed to become the Patron, an important event which earned this simple minute in the Club's records: 'Letter from HRH Duke of Connaught agreeing to become Patron'. He was followed in 1942 by the Duke of Gloucester and now by his son, the present Duke.

Here is what the Duke of Connaught replied to the Club's request for his patronage:

BAGSHOT
28th October 1888

Dear Major McKenzie,
I have just heard from H.R.H. the Duke of Connaught, to say that he will be very pleased to become Patron of the golf Club.
Yours faithfully,
(signed) H. ELPHINSTONE
Major McKenzie
The Warren
Loughton

Later in the same year, 1888, the Home Office, in response to a request from the Club's Captain, Mr F. G. Faithfull, for the royal title, replied that the Queen was agreeable to the royal title being granted, in these terms:

Secretary of State
Home Department,
Whitehall.
30th November 1888

Sir,
Referring to the Memorial forwarded to this Department for permission to use the title 'Royal' in connection with the name of the 'Epping Forest Golf Club' I am directed by the Secretary of State to inform you that he has laid the application before the Queen, and that Her Majesty has been graciously pleased to comply with the request, and to command that the Club in question shall be called the 'Royal Epping Forest Golf Club.'
I am, Sir,
Your obedient Servant,
(signed) GODFREY LUSHINGTON
G. F. Faithfull Esq M.A.
Merchant Taylors' Hall
Threadneedle Street E.C.

Coming to more recent times, the Club and course were in the front line of the Battle of Britain and the subsequent Blitz. The Honourable Artillery Company deployed its anti-aircraft guns here, and the RAF fighters from North Weald and Hornchurch were prominent in gaining victory.

The Club's history reports two incidents of those famous days which caught my eye:

> In February 1940 it was resolved that ARP Wardens should be permitted to use the Club if they so desired, but in July 1941 the shortage of beer caused the Club to ask Wardens not to visit the bar so frequently.

And later this uncompromising directive:

> The shortage of whisky resulted in a minute in December 1951, 'That no visitors be served with whisky until further notice.'

ROYAL WEST NORFOLK GOLF CLUB, BRANCASTER

This grand old links has had royal patronage from its earliest beginnings. According to the late Pat Ward Thomas, the distinguished golf writer, who loved this place, the Prince of Wales, later King Edward VII, was shooting snipe on the marshes near Sandringham and his companion Holcombe Ingleby remarked that the links land would be ideal for golf. Soon afterwards the golf club was formed and the course laid out by Ingleby with the help of Horace Hutchinson, one of the

The Prince of Wales, later Edward VIII, captain of the Royal and Ancient Golf Club of St Andrews, 1922. Portrait by Sir William Orpen, RA (by courtesy of the R&A)

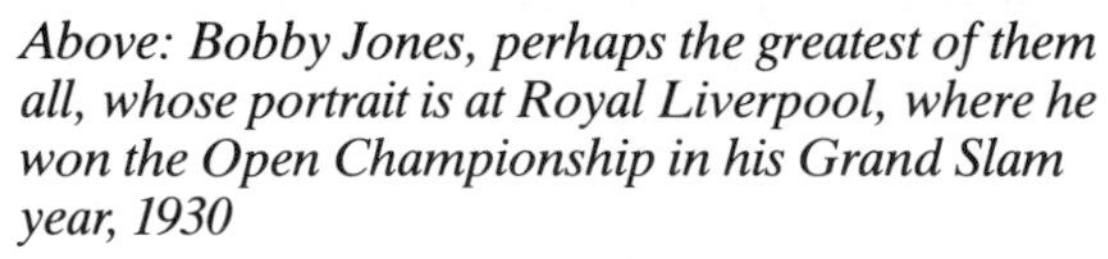

Above: Bobby Jones, perhaps the greatest of them all, whose portrait is at Royal Liverpool, where he won the Open Championship in his Grand Slam year, 1930

Top right: J.H. Taylor, five times Open champion, whose portrait hangs in the club house of the Royal North Devon Club at Westward Ho!

Right: Pam Barton, winner of the British and United States Ladies' Championships in 1936 at the age of nineteen, whose portrait hangs in the club house of Royal Mid-Surrey. A Flight Officer in the WAAF, she died in a plane crash during World War II

Henry Cotton, winner of the Open Championship three times, the first golfer to be honoured with a knighthood shortly before his death in 1988

The Great Triumvirate – J.H. Taylor, James Braid and Harry Vardon – who between them won sixteen of the twenty-one Open Championships between 1894 and 1914

Left: The Royal Burgess Golfing Society of Edinburgh, the only society or club to have celebrated its 250th anniversary – the gathering are celebrating the occasion in 1985

Below: The Royal Birkdale links on the Lancashire coast where Peter Thomson in 1965 and Tom Watson in 1983 each won the Open Championship for the fifth time

Above: The Mountains of Mourne provide a glorious backdrop to the splendid links of Royal County Down in Northern Ireland

Below: The 18th green at Royal Lytham and St Annes, where Severiano Ballesteros won the Open Championship in 1979 (pictured) and 1988

Above: The Royal Jersey Club in the Channel Isles, birthplace of famous golfers, notably Harry Vardon

Below: A view of the 6th green at Royal St George's, Sandwich, from the great sandhill, the Maiden

Royal Troon, venue of the 1989 Open Championship, has the shortest hole in championship golf, the 8th, named the Postage Stamp

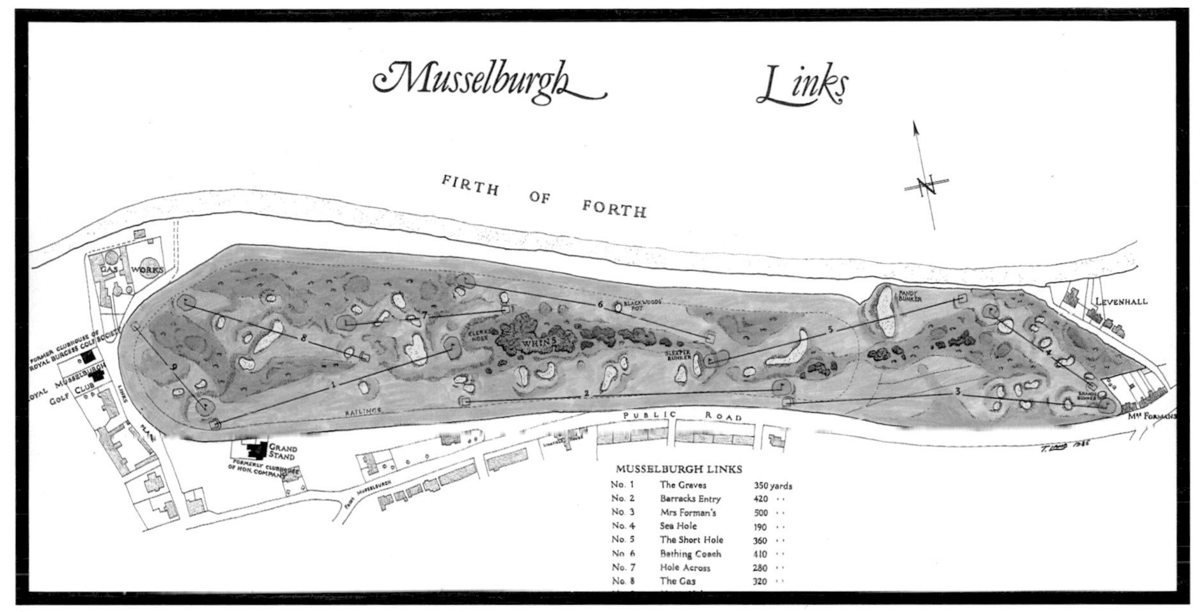

Above: A plan of Musselburgh links

Below: The splendid links of Royal West Norfolk at Brancaster are captured in this fine painting by Julian Barrow (Burlington Galleries)

The oldest royal golf club is the Royal Perth Golfing Society and County and City Club, whose members play on the public course at North Inch (author pictured)

Below: Royal Cromer features a lighthouse on the edge of the course and fine views of the town and sea

A painting of the 17th hole at St Andrews was chosen for a poster by the London and North Eastern railway

Above: The 18th green at Royal St George's in 1985 as Sandy Lyle became Open champion

Left: Royal Dublin, founded in 1886, still retains its royal title

The club house of the Royal Johannesburg club, with the jacaranda trees in full bloom

Left: The 15th green at Royal Montreal, the oldest golf club in North America

Below: The 18th hole of the Eden Course at the Royal Hong Kong Golf Club

Royal Melbourne has two splendid courses – pictured is the 5th hole on the West Course

Above: A view of the Royal Malta course

Below: The club house of the Royal Belgian club, the Chateau of Ravenstein, over 200 years old

Real Club de la Puerto de Hierro in Madrid, the premier club of Spain, pictured from the northern outskirts of the capital

Left: The Royal Nepal Club at Kathmandu

Below: The club house of the Royal and Ancient Golf Club of St Andrews

A print of a famous picture – the golfers of Blackheath. The original has been lost

Left: King Hassan II of Morocco is a keen golfer and has done much for the game in his country

Below: The King and Queen of Spain show a keen interest in the Spanish Open Championship, and are seen here with Sandy Lyle and tennis player, Manuel Santana

leading amateur players of the day. That was in 1891, and the Club sprang royally into life with the Prince of Wales as Patron and the royal title granted. In those days personal contact counted for a great deal.

The royal patronage has continued, with King George V succeeding his father, followed in turn by his two sons, Edward VIII and George VI, and today the Duke of Edinburgh. If this were not enough, the Duke of Gloucester, King George V's third son, was Captain in 1928, his elder brother, the Prince of Wales in 1929, and his younger brother, the Duke of Kent, in 1937. A pleasant sequel to this has been the present Duke of Kent's captaincy in 1981.

A notable event, recorded by Ward Thomas in *Country Life*, took place on Whit Monday in 1931, when the Prince of Wales and his brothers Gloucester and Kent played in a match against the Brancaster Village Club. Edward P won both his matches, George and Henry playing together lost their foursome, but the Duke of Kent won his single handsomely.

The course at Brancaster, though at times sorely beset by the sea, remains very much as it was laid out in 1891 amid the dunes and marshes close to the shore. Some substantial changes were made by Major C. K. Hutchinson in 1928–9 and some further modifications after World War II, made necessary by the encroaching sea. Uncompromising cross-bunkers, nowadays regarded as old-fashioned, often revetted by wooden palisades of old railway sleepers, are a feature and demand the proper shots. Narrow fairways, deep hazards, thin, spare turf, small and keen greens and at intervals the marshlands on the inward side filling with the tide – all combine to show us linkslands golf at its simple, unmanipulated best, something from the past perhaps but agreeable to those who believe in letting well alone. The marsh itself provides a splendid home for sea-birds and wild flowers.

May I be excused for quoting what I said in *Play the Best Courses*?

> Have I given the impression that Brancaster is impossibly severe, too harsh in its punishments and too brutal with its cross-bunkering and ancient style? I hope not, for in fine weather it can be amazingly beautiful, the sea birds wheeling and crying overhead, the marsh with its own flowers and perhaps after a blow the sea making a continuous roar on the sands out of sight beyond the rampart of dunes. Remote, serene and unspoilt, may it long continue.

ROYAL WORLINGTON AND NEWMARKET GOLF CLUB

There are many reasons why this club should be famous. First, there are only 9 holes – but they make the best 9-hole golf-course in the world; some go even further and say they are the best 9-hole layout in the world or even that they are the nine best individual holes.

I would not go that far but be content to accept the experts' judgements. Thus Bernard Darwin, our greatest writer on the game, spoke of 'the sacred nine of Worlington'. Herbert Warren Wind, America's leading writer on the game, who understands golf in Britain with such perception, wrote in the *New Yorker* in 1981: 'it is far and away the best nine hole course in the world, and it also held that position in the distant days before the First World War, when the nine hole course was in flower'. Donald Steel has written: 'Worlington's greatness lies in a basic simplicity that permeates everything about it, including a club house whose convivial character appeals to those who believe informality more important than the sumptuous grandeur of other settings.'

I can say amen to this last, as the Vice-President and the Secretary saw me on my way most handsomely with some splendid port when I visited the Club to seek information the other day.

At this point I feel I must insert another quotation from Herb Wind's article:

> The most popular drink at Worlington on gala occasions – such as the annual stroke-play competition for the Captain's Prize – is a concoction called a Pink Jug, because it was originally mixed in a pink jug. The recipe calls for one bottle of French champagne . . . one measure each of Benedictine, Brandy and Pimms No. 1; and ice and lemon. In a country in which the old club tie still carries considerable clout, Worlington's tie is navy blue with a single pink jug.

The second good reason for fame at Worlington is the quality of the ground itself. A small area of sandy, fast-draining soil amid the heavy land surrounding it has led to a dry, fast, quick-draining course with fast, lively greens.

A third plus for the club is, in my eyes, fully deserved, and that is the desire to 'hold fast to that which is good' and preserve the best style and traditions of amateur golf. The small, unchanged club house, the course virtually untampered with for eighty years and yet able to offer such a fine round to play today, the prohibition of 3- and 4-ball matches, the resolute refusal to use less suitable land to turn Worlington into an 18-hole course – all these point the same way, rather old-fashioned and behind the times it may seem, but for many it gives a placid, serene and enjoyable environment. As a further mark of renown, Worlington is the home green of the Cambridge University golf team.

The last claim to fame of Worlington is, of course, that it is the only 9-hole royal club.

A description of the course itself is out of place here, but I would say that seven out of nine holes are first-class, two are very adequate, while the short 5th, without a single bunker, and the long par-4 8th, with a huge cross-bunker across the fairway, are excellent. Golf was played here a few years before the course was properly laid out and the Club formed in 1893; then, taking advantage of the natural features of the ground, including a long straight belt of Scots pines, a very compact round was created. The famous golf architect Harry Colt, who had earlier been Captain of the Cambridge team, made modifications in 1906, lengthening the 1st and 3rd holes and 'converting the 9th from a lack-lustre par-3 to a great short par-4'. This is the course that survives to this day.

Royal honours came early to the Club, application to the Home Secretary on 8 June 1894 receiving this response:

> Secretary of State
> Home Department
> B 18668 WHITEHALL
> 3rd July 1895
>
> Sir
>
> With reference to your letter of the 8th ultimo applying for permission to make use of the title 'Royal' in the name of the Worlington and Newmarket Golf Club, I am directed by the Secretary of State to inform you that he has laid your application before the Queen and that Her Majesty has been graciously pleased to accede to your request, and to command that the Worlington and Newmarket Golf Club shall be called the 'Royal Worlington and Newmarket Golf Club'.
>
> With regard to your application for permission to make use of the Prince of Wales Feathers as the crest, I am to say that you should address yourself to Sir Francis Knollys, Marlborough House.
>
> (signature unascertainable)

And this response from the Prince of Wales's secretary:

> Marlborough House
> Pall Mall
> SW
> 6th July 1895
>
> Sir
>
> I have submitted your letter of the 4th instant to the Prince of Wales. His Royal Highness desires me to inform you in reply

Right: The opening of the full course at Royal Norwich in 1894

that he will be happy to allow his Feathers to appear in the coat of Arms of the Club, but that he is unable to grant permission that they should form the entire crest.

I am sir
Your obedient servant
(Sgd.) FRANCIS KNOLLYS

THE ROYAL NORWICH GOLF CLUB

Golf here got off to a galloping start. In a few short weeks from 21 August 1893, when a letter in a local paper called for a club to be formed, matters went with a rush. A preliminary meeting, followed by one in the city Guildhall chaired by the Mayor, led to the forming of a club, the appointment of officers, the building of a club house, the purchase of land at Hellesdon and the opening of a 9-hole course, all by St Andrew's Day, 30 November. A second 9-hole layout followed by 1 February 1894, a professional was appointed, and a grand opening took place with a professional exhibition match between Douglas Rolland, the mighty hitter, and little Ben Sayers.

Later that year, after the tragic drama of the Abdication, we can read:

PRIVY PURSE OFFICE
BUCKINGHAM PALACE
S.W.

MEMORANDUM

The Keeper of the Privy Purse is commanded by the King* to state that His Majesty is pleased to intimate to those Societies and Institutions which were recently granted Patronage by King Edward VIII that they may continue to show the Sovereign as their Patron during the present reign unless otherwise notified.

14th December 1936

The course of the Royal Norwich Club is in parkland astride the Drayton Road on the outskirts of the city. The layout was drastically overhauled by James Braid in 1924, and his commonsense style is apparent today and has stood the test of time. There are good trees, and the sandy soil with slopes and folds gives an enjoyable round.

The fine new club house dates from 1964, and is located on a new site which necessitated renumbering of the holes. Its opening ceremony was performed by Arthur Havers, Open Champion in 1923, one of the few British winners of the Championship in the 1920s. Havers, with whom I once had the pleasure of a game at Coombe Hill, was born in Hellesdon, the son of a former steward, within a stone's throw of the new club house.

The first President, Mr J. J. Colman MP, of mustard fame, had opened the course, and it was no doubt he, though no records persist, who negotiated the grant of royal patronage and the royal title for the Club with the Duke of York, who later became King George V. So, like other East Anglian clubs, Royal Norwich gained almost instant royal status.

The royal title was confirmed by papers preserved in the club house which read as follows:

PRIVY PURSE OFFICE
BUCKINGHAM PALACE
S.W.

15th July 1936

Dear Sir

I am commanded by the King* to inform you that His Majesty has been graciously pleased to grant his Patronage to the Royal Norwich Golf Club.

Yours truly.

Wigram
Keeper of the Privy Purse

The President
Royal Norwich Golf Club

* George VI.

* Edward VIII.

CHAPTER 7

Later English royal clubs

The clubs that come into this chapter are these, in order of their foundation:

1	Royal Lytham and St Annes	1886
2	Royal Ascot	1887
3	Royal Eastbourne	
4	Royal St George's, Sandwich	
5	Royal Ashdown Forest	1888
6	Royal Winchester	
7	Royal Birkdale	1889
8	Royal Cinque Ports, Deal	1892
9	Royal Mid-Surrey	

Before embarking on the stories of these nine clubs, we should note the exclusions from this list and the drop-outs. We have left out clubs whose names embody the word 'Royal' for reasons unconnected with golf – such as the Royal Automobile Club, which provides for its members 36 holes of attractive golf at its country club in Surrey, where, incidentally, I saw for the only time the incomparable Bobby Jones in action, sixty years ago. Similarly clubs under the wing of the Royal Air Force are omitted. Out too are clubs attached to places with a royal name such as Bognor Regis, Studeley Royal and the Royal Forest of Dean.

Royal clubs of genuine texture which have departed this life include the Royal Isle of Wight Golf Club, the Royal Eastbourne Ladies' and the Royal Ashdown Forest Ladies' Golf Clubs, which will be discussed later, and the Royal Cornwall Golf Club.

The Cornish club was founded in 1889 as the Cornwall County Golf Club, with 9 holes on Bodmin Old Race Course, on Bodmin Moor. It apparently became the *Royal Cornwall Golf Club* in 1891, together with the Royal Cornwall Ladies' Golf Club, from the patronage of the Prince of Wales, who also bore the title of Duke of Cornwall. The Club continued until World War II, when play ceased. The greens still survive on the moor, but the old club house became a café. The Club remained nominally in being, with a committee which met annually to preserve the name, until the last year or so, transferring its trophies on permanent loan to the Cornwall Golf Union, but activity now seems to have ceased. Mr Alan Gawler and Mr Stanley Martin have been most helpful in gathering this information for us.

ROYAL LYTHAM AND ST ANNES

This famous Lancashire club has just celebrated its centenary, but it was not until just before it held its first Open Championship in 1926 that it received the royal title.

The Club was formed in 1886 by a local group and started play on land to the north of the present links, moving to the present site in 1897. Part of the old site is now occupied by another club, St Annes Old Links. The land on which Royal Lytham plays was part of the great estates of the Clifton family, who had been squires of Lytham Hall since 1606, and John Talbot Clifton was the first President of the Club. He was succeeded by his nephew Talbot Clifton, of whom more in a moment, whose wife Violet Clifton was involved, we read in the Club's admirable book *The Lytham Century*, in the granting of the royal title in 1926:

> In May, His Majesty, King George V was graciously pleased to command that we should henceforth be known as the 'Royal Lytham and St. Anne's Golf Club'. No mention of this

Bobby Jones and Al Watrous playing in the Open Championship at Royal Lytham and St Annes in 1926

is made in Pym Williamson's economical Council minutes, but 'The Book of Talbot', written by Mrs. Violet Clifton, wife of our President, says: 'From across the Atlantic famous golfers came to play on the course and Talbot and Violet [Clifton] were able, through the influence of "one in a high place", to have the designation of "Royal" conferred by Charter.' Since Mrs. Clifton was a close personal friend of Her Majesty Queen Mary and was often invited to take tea with her at Buckingham Palace, we can draw our own conclusions whom she was writing about.

The following description of the Club President at this time, also from the Club's record, is too good to omit:

This extract from Oliver St. John Gogarty's book, published by the Hutchinson Publishing Group Ltd., 'As I was going down Sackville Street', describes Talbot Clifton as 'noble, aimless, irascible, bullying, dauntless, extravagant, generous, scorning craftiness or thrift, golden-hearted, golden-fisted, fast to his friends, sadistical and successful. He stood 6′ 4″ tall and straight, a blue-eyed giant with a golden beard – the greatest extrovert and the mightiest sportsman in the world.' A man of great wealth, on one of his explorations to the ends of the world, he was short of money and sent a message to his trustees 'Sell Blackpool'. Of course, this could not be done as the estate was entailed. President from 1890 until 1928, he designed his own uniform. The scarlet tail coat was similar to that worn by our Captains but the lapels were faced with light blue silk.

Master Edward Fisher had the misfortune to caddie for him, when he sliced a ball into the pond at the first hole. He immediately ordered Edward: 'Go in and get it, boy.' But Edward had a new suit on and being even more scared of his parents' wrath than the Squire's, he refused. The Squire finished his round and had lunch. Afterwards he called all the caddies together and ordered them to get his ball, but none would. In a rage he took out a handful of sovereigns and threw them into the pond and they went in. When he was 25, Edward was appointed Gamekeeper to the squire and lived in Keeper's Cottage, near Cross Slack Cottage, where he was born.

Caddie Jack Pearson said, 'The Squire was a hell of a big fellow and a bad b—r. If he drove into the rough in his rage he grabbed you and shaked you like a rabbit.' All the caddies were terrified of him and when they saw his car come over St. Thomas's bridge, they hid in the bushes and there wasn't one in sight, when he arrived. He had a German Chauffeur with size 14 boots. Often Mrs. Violet Clifton, a big handsome woman, walked around with him.

One day the Squire bought a set of new clubs. Losing a £5 bet on his game, he threw them into the pond and driving home hell for leather, having just bought one of the first motor cars, was fined for speeding, when the limit was 20 miles per hour. Before this he was to be seen in a high dog cart with his groom perched precariously behind, driving tandem at a hard gallop and turning into the Club entrance with accuracy on one wheel.

Another attractive fact to emerge from *The Lytham Century* is that Robert Boddington, who was Captain in 1896–8, would arrive at the Club driving his own four-in-hand with his coachman called Alcock on the box. Alcock's son, Sir John Alcock, with Sir Arthur Whitten Brown, were the first men to fly direct across the Atlantic.

Quoting from my own *Play the Best Courses*:

In the 100 years since golf started here the district has suffered major changes and what was once a piece of mixed agriculture and

Tony Jacklin, first British winner of the Open for eighteen years, at Royal Lytham and St Annes in 1969

linksland, bounded by the railway and blown over by wild breezes and flying sand from the dunes along the shore, is now an oasis in the wilderness of modern housing in the great conurbation of Blackpool and St Annes.

Inevitably the character of the course has changed in this process, as has that of so many of the great seaside links, and it has become more 'inland'. With a desire for better lies and softer greens, water and fertiliser have been applied and much of the bone-hardness once so characteristic of St Andrews, Hoylake and here have gone for ever, but Royal Lytham and St Annes remains a great course and it is now firmly established in the Championship rota. The Open came here in 1926, 1952, 1958, 1963 and again in 1969 when Tony Jacklin won his famous victory – the first win by a British player since 1951. The Open was here again in 1974 when Gary Player, the winner, played a left-handed shot from the side of the club

Princess Alexandra presents the Ryder Cup at Royal Lytham in 1977 to US captain, Dow Finsterwald

house and in 1979 and is due in 1988. The Amateur was here in 1935, 1955 and 1968 and the Ryder Cup in 1961 and 1977.

In the mists of the past the first Ladies' Championship was played here; here Bobby Jones won his first British Open in 1926 in a dramatic finish after a day-long struggle with Al Watrous and here the first left-hander to win a major competition, Bob Charles of New Zealand, triumphed in 1963 after a tie. The first win for Spain came in 1979 when young Ballesteros beat off the Americans with his brilliant recovery shots and beautiful putting touch.

The course is rather flat, especially at the club-house end, and many of the 'seaside' hillocks and dunes are in fact the work of man not nature, fashioned by countless spades and cartloads long before the days of the bulldozer but done with a skill which matches the folds and bumps of the natural linksland across the railway nearer the shore.

Say what you like about the course, on one facet of this great club all are agreed, and that is the great warmth and hospitality which have from time immemorial always been bestowed on the visitor. Let Gerald Micklem in his foreword to *The Lytham Century* speak for us all. He says:

> What is it that sets 'Royal Lytham' apart from its fellows after its first hundred years? It is its hospitality, both corporate and personal. One has only to read Bernard Darwin's account of the Oxford & Cambridge Golfing Society tours in the early days of the century to see how well visitors were entertained, and the same spirit continues to the present day. Northern hospitality has always been famous and 'Royal Lytham' leads the way.

ROYAL ASCOT

Ascot Heath has been part of the Crown Lands for over 250 years, and horse-racing here goes back to the days of Queen Anne. Other sports followed, and the area enclosed by the race-course has been used for golf and cricket for over a hundred years.

In 1883 Queen Victoria granted permission for cricket to be played here and allowed the players to style themselves the Royal Ascot Cricket Club, a rare, if not a unique distinction for cricketers. In 1887 on the initiative of a local lawyer, F. J. Patton, a golf club was proposed. Queen Victoria, in granting permission for the formation, allowed it to be named the Royal Ascot Golf Club. This then is one of the oldest royal golf clubs in England. Unfortunately little information on the early days of the Club exists beyond what is published in the Club's excellent little centenary history. All the Club's early records were lost in a fire over fifteen years ago.

When King Edward VII came to the throne in 1901 he continued the royal patronage of the Club and the use of the royal title.

The course comes under the benevolent rule of the Ascot Authority, which rents the whole property from the Crown and controls all activities on the Heath. The race-course having priority as it were, the golf-course has undergone many changes of layout, notably when the two jump-courses were added in 1965. Nevertheless an attractive heathland course of 18 holes inside the encircling racetracks survives, and in spite of its limited length, 5653 yards, it gives an amusing and pleasant round with plenty of man-made hazards among those provided by nature. Furze and bush prevail in the rough, but unfortunately, in the interests of television, big trees have been abolished. The first serious layout here was in 1895 by the great J. H. Taylor, who was, in those gutty days, a believer in such uncompromising hazards as bunkers across the line of play. Some traces of this vigorous, straightforward style still exist on the course, notably at the 11th, near the ground of the Royal Ascot Cricket Club, which is guarded by a cross-bunker in front of the green.

Golf on Ascot Heath continued with moderate success, suffering with its limitations from the competition of the more famous local clubs at Sunningdale, Swinley Forest, Wentworth and the Berkshire. The Club, however, was dealt a mortal blow by World War I, and finally in 1922 it sank beneath the waves, taking its royal title with it.

Golf continued on the Heath under the aegis of the Ascot Authority, who kept up the course and allowed play to continue. Then in 1947 enough interest was aroused for a new members' club, under the name of the Ascot Heath Golf Club, to be formed with the help and blessing of the Authority.

In 1977, the Jubilee Year, after some internal controversy, the Ascot Heath Club, through its President, Captain the Hon. Nicholas Beaumont, Clerk of the Course and Secretary to the Ascot Authority, applied to the Queen through the Home Office for reinstatement as the Royal Ascot Golf Club. To the surprise of many and the delight of all, the petition was granted, so reviving the old title which had been sleeping, if not dead, for fifty-five years. The letters exchanged between Captain Beaumont and the Home Office were these:

28th July, 1977

R. D. Shuffrey, Esq.,
Under Secretary of State,
The Home Office,
Whitehall,
LONDON, S.W.1.

The Ascot Heath Golf Club

The Ascot Authority are the landlords of the Ascot Heath Golf Club. They have had a request from the Club that it may once again be called the 'Royal Ascot Golf Club'.

I enclose a handbook which shows that the Club originally was called the Royal Ascot Golf Club but, looking through the records, the Authority cannot find out when the word

'Royal' was dropped, or why. I would be very grateful if the handbook could be returned at your convenience as it appears to be the only one in existence.

The Ascot Heath Golf Club wish to have their own Club flag and Club tie and have asked if a Crown can be incorporated in the design. This design would, of course, have to be approved by the Ascot Authority to see that it was suitable.

There is a Royal Ascot Cricket Club and a Royal Ascot Tennis Club at Ascot and the Authority hope that the name 'Royal' may be restored to the Ascot Golf Club.

[Letter from Captain the Hon. E. N. C. Beaumont MVO, Clerk of the Course and Secretary to the Ascot Authority]

30 August 1977

Captain the Hon. E N C Beaumont MVO
Clerk of the Course and Secretary
to the Ascot Authority
Royal Enclosure
ASCOT
Berks

Dear Captain Beaumont

You wrote on 28 July about the use of the title 'Royal' by the Ascot Heath Golf Club.

Our records show that the Ascot Golf Club was granted permission to use the title 'Royal' by Queen Victoria in 1887 (the year of its foundation) and that this permission was confirmed by King Edward VII in 1901. In the circumstances there would be no objection to the Club resuming the use of the title 'Royal Ascot Golf Club'.

The use of a Royal Crown on the Club's flag and tie would require the consent of The Queen, who is advised on such matters by the Home Secretary. Permission is rarely given and in this case I regret that the Home Secretary would be unable, consistently with the established practice in these matters, to make a favourable recommendation to Her Majesty.

The handbook and map which you kindly sent me are returned herewith.

Yours sincerely
(Sgd) RALPH SHUFFREY
(R F D SHUFFREY)

Perhaps the most notable events in the history of the Royal Ascot Golf Club outside its own affairs have been the British Ladies' Championship here in 1959 and the promotion in that hot dry summer of 1921 and again in 1922 of the first International Boys' Championship, an event which today requires the attention of no less an organizer than the Royal & Ancient. Among the competitors in that pioneering event was fourteen-year-old Henry Cotton, later thrice Open Champion, his elder brother Leslie and my old friend and fellow-Harrovian Raymond Oppenheimer, who later won the CBE for his services to golf and became a world authority on bull-terriers. The winner of that tournament was Donald Mathieson, who beat Guy Lintott at the 37th hole in the final. Donald Mathieson, who won again in 1923, was still going strong at the time of writing. Henry Cotton MBE was the Guest of Honour at the Royal Ascot Club's centenary celebrations early in July 1987, eighty years old and full of spirit, according to my most helpful host at the Club, the Secretary, Mr R. J. Young, but the sad news of his death just before Christmas 1987 has since overtaken the celebrations. It is good to know that Henry's knighthood was known to him before he died, and that it was posthumously conferred, so that golf's first knight can take his place in sport along with Sir Gordon, Sir Jack, Sir Donald, Sir Leonard and Sir Stanley.

ROYAL EASTBOURNE

The spick and span town of Eastbourne owes much of its quality to the Cavendish family – allied to the Compton family in time past – under the 7th Duke of Devonshire, who inspired and created the fine, well-planned town we know today.

Golf was brought to Eastbourne in 1887 by the efforts of a local solicitor and member of the R & A, Arthur Mayhewe, who gained the necessary support of the Duke of Devonshire and his two sons, the Marquis of Hartington and Lord Edward Cavendish, to allow play to take place on the Links, an area of open grassland so called long before golf came to the area. The original 9 holes were designed by Horace Hutchinson, the current Amateur Champion, and these, with 18 additions, form the course today. The nature of the ground is pure downland turf on chalk, under the shelter of the South Downs, a couple of miles before they plunge into the sea at Beachy Head. The golf is agreeable, without pretensions to be of 'championship' calibre (a claim too often made today by clubs unworthy of such a description) – a most attractive course.

I found it of interest that cricket was reported as being played here in 1738, in that Eastbourne's opponents came from my home town of Battle.

The Eastbourne Golf Club started life supported by a tremendous battery of swells, the Duke of Devonshire as President, Viscount Hampden, the Earl of Ashburnham and Lord Edward Cavendish among the Vice-Presidents, the Marquis of Hartington as Captain, and Horace Hutchinson and Lord Vernon from Royal Wimbledon on the Council. It is small wonder that royal patronage and the royal title were almost immediately gained. Let the historian of the club, John Milton, who writes so well, tell us in his own words from the Club's history:

> The Hon. Secretary lost no time in seeking Royal patronage for the Club as soon as it was established and received a letter from Fredensborg Castle, Denmark dated 11th October 1887.
>
> Sir,
>
> I am desired by Prince Albert Victor of Wales to say that it will give His Royal Highness much pleasure to become patron of the Eastbourne Golf Club.
>
> I regret that owing to my absence abroad I have been unable to return an earlier answer.
>
> Believe me,
>
> Yours faithfully,
>
> A. Greville

Prince Albert Victor, Duke of Clarence, was the elder son of the Prince of Wales. He was then aged 23 and died only five years later.

Before the end of that same month an even more important letter was received:

> Whitehall
>
> 27 October 1887
>
> Sir,
>
> I am directed by Mr. Secretary Matthews to inform you that he has had the honour to lay before the Queen the application of the Eastbourne Golf Club to be permitted to use the title 'Royal' in connection with the name of the club and that Her Majesty has been pleased to accede to the prayer of the Memorial and to command that the club in question shall be styled 'The Royal Eastbourne Golf Club'.
>
> I am, Sir,
>
> Your obedient servant,
>
> Godfrey Lushington
>
> A. Mayhewe Esq.,
> Kilvington
> Eastbourne

Such is the Club's authority to bear the title which it has proudly carried ever since. At the time Henry Matthews was Secretary of State and Godfrey Lushington was Permanent Under-Secretary, Home Department.

The author has traced no other golf club that obtained its Royal title so soon after birth.* At the other extreme Troon was honoured on the occasion of its centenary and the Burgess Golfing Society of Edinburgh was nearly two hundred years old before becoming 'Royal'. What was special about Eastbourne? Firstly, it is a true saying in many circumstances that if you don't ask you don't get. Secondly, having

* Not so: some of the clubs in East Anglia, for example, can match this.

asked, you need powerful support. This was clearly forthcoming from a Ducal President and such a Captain as the Marquis of Hartington. Hartington was, at that time, one of the most influential men in the country, well known to and respected by the Queen as well as being the leader of 78 Liberal Unionist M.P.s whose support was essential to a Conservative government. Any organisation with which he was concerned had a very good start.

It is indeed likely that Lord Hartington's support was given. He was a close friend of the Prince of Wales (later Edward VII) and known in royal circles as 'Harty-Tarty'.

The Club's first Royal Patron died in 1892 and was succeeded in office by his younger brother George, Duke of Cornwall and York later to become Prince of Wales after his father had come to the throne. In 1906 King Edward VII himself honoured the Club by becoming Patron in place of his son. Although the author has found no proof that the King ever played on the course, he certainly did play golf both in this country and on the Continent and if he did so at Eastbourne while staying with the 8th Duke at Compton Place this could account for the change of Patronage at that time.

After the death of his father in 1910 the new King, George V, became Patron of the Club once again and remained so until his death in 1936.

King Edward VIII made it a rule that he would only grant Patronage to clubs with which he had been associated as Prince of Wales and George VI worked on the same general principle. Letters from Buckingham Palace addressed to the then Marquis of Hartington make this point on behalf of both Kings and so the club has had no further Royal Patronage. One of these letters dated 4th August 1936 makes clear in its last paragraph a point over which there is sometimes confusion. It states '. . . the title "Royal" has not therefore to be given up. The two privileges are in fact quite separate.'

To finish the royal narrative of the Eastbourne Club, here is another quotation from chronicler Milton:

On 9th December 1893 the *Eastbourne Chronicle* proudly reported:
The Ladies Golf Club – Her Royal Highness, the Duchess of Fife has graciously consented to become Patroness of the Ladies Golf Club which will henceforth be styled the 'Royal Eastbourne Ladies Golf Club'.
Princess Louise, Duchess of Fife was the third child and eldest daughter of the Prince of Wales and was created Princess Royal by her father, then King Edward VII, in 1905 at the age of 38.

[We have of course met the Princess Royal in our Scottish chapter and also at Royal Craggan]:

A retiring figure who played only a small part in public life and was nicknamed 'Her Royal Shyness', she and her husband had a seaside residence at Kemp Town, Brighton from where they paid occasional visits to Compton Place. The Duchess took up golf about 1900 when it is reported that she was taking lessons and playing at East Brighton G.C. but it is doubtful if she ever played at Eastbourne. She died in 1931, 19 years after the death of the Duke following a shipwreck off the North African coast in which they were both involved.

This Royal title bestowed upon the R.E.L.G.C. makes it in all probability the first and one of only two or three independent ladies' golf clubs ever to be so honoured. Forty years later* when the Ladies' Section was formed the Club Secretary of R.E.G.C. was instructed to write to the Ladies' Club stating that it was no longer entitled to use the royal title. No doubt the men thought at that time that the title had just been casually adopted because of the close relationship between the two clubs. The Council minutes do not record

* In 1933; the RELGC ceased to exist in 1937.

what answer was received by the Secretary but convincing evidence for the right to use the title was presumably produced because thereafter the R.E.L.G.C. is always referred to as such. On 17th March 1937 the *Eastbourne Gazette* in a report on the Ladies' Club stated that it 'enjoys the title of Royal by virtue of a charter granted by Queen Victoria'. Unfortunately, this 'charter', which would probably have been just a letter of assent, has disappeared together with all other prime documentary evidence concerning the Ladies' Club.

ROYAL ST GEORGE'S, SANDWICH

We now come to a very famous and very fine golf club, the Royal St George's at Sandwich, which with its only slightly less illustrious neighbour at Deal has had a special place in my memories and my affections since my own first acquaintance over sixty years ago.

So I was delighted to be able to attend the Club's centenary celebrations in May 1987 – in weather of an almost obscene malignity – and immensely proud to have been honoured with a quotation among all the other eulogies noted in the Club's centenary handbook; proud too for the words of mine chosen – striking a different note from praise of the course lavished by others – which said:

> There is a pleasant conservative air about the place, and the clubhouse, save for the elimination of sandboxes and earth closets, is as it always has been. A relaxed peaceful leather-furnished smoking-room persists and you can still get a tankard of ale from the wood. I have detected only one change for the worse; you now have to pay for matches.

Away now from self-praise to a few words about this great links. It is first and foremost of the true metal, links golf at its best, great sandhills, narrow valleys, greens in dells or on plateaux, severe carries, flat, uncompromising areas and solitude of the most enjoyable kind; you can only see the hole you are playing – and not always all of that. All great courses require good driving and none more than Sandwich; it is indeed, as has been said, a driver's course: if you can't get clear from the tee there is no redress.

The course has been altered from time to time, and the most recent changes, put in hand to make possible Sandwich's triumphal return to the Open Championship rota in 1981, have greatly improved it. It does not fit the pattern of this book to take you round the links, so we will rest with the quotation from Walter Hagen, who won the Open here in 1922 and again in 1928: 'The first nine holes – tremendous fun, not very good golf. Second nine holes – tremendous golf, no fun at all'; and with Frank Pennink's 'One of the great links of England with one of the toughest finishing stretches of any championship links'; and lastly from Bernard Darwin, the Master, who wrote: 'a fine spring day, with the larks singing as they seem to sing nowhere else; the sun shining on the waters of Pegwell Bay and lighting up the white cliffs in the distance, this is as nearly my idea of heaven as is to be attained on any earthly links'.

Hardly had Sandwich opened than major

The Great Triumvirate of Harry Vardon, J.H. Taylor and James Braid, who all won the Open Championship on royal courses

The Prince of Wales at the 1928 Open Championship at Sandwich, presenting the trophy to the winner Walter Hagen

honours came thick and fast. In 1892 the Amateur Championship was held here for the first time in the South of England, and in 1894 the Open for the first time outside Scotland. This was also the first Open won by an English professional, J. H. Taylor, who won with 326 strokes; out of the field of ninety-four players only two rounds beat 80. Both Championships have been here many times since, although the Open passed by for thirty-two years. Twice Sandwich has seen a British win in the Open after a long period of overseas success: in 1934, when Henry Cotton played super golf, and in 1985 when Sandy Lyle just pulled it off with a brave 70 to finish.

An early event which attracted the best amateur players was and is the St George's Champion Grand Challenge Cup. Play began in 1888, and winners range from such old giants as John Ball and Harold Hilton to Jack Nicklaus, who was still an amateur in 1959, and Michael Bonallack.

The Walker Cup against the American Amateurs has been here twice. An interesting fact about the Walker Cup has been discovered by Donald Steel, who writes for the *Sunday Telegraph*. He finds that Herbert Walker, who gave the Cup, was the maternal grandfather of George Herbert Walker Bush, who was elected President of the United States in 1988. But surely the most unusual event was the proposal, later turned down, to hold the Olympic Games golf tournament here in 1908. Lord Desborough, President of the British Olympic Committee, invited the club to manage the Golf Section.

Right: *The Open Championship at Sandwich in 1894, won by J.H. Taylor, pictured top left*

Sandy Lyle, winning the 1985 Open at Sandwich

This raised protests from St Andrews, who thought that golf was not suitable for the Olympics and that if it was they should manage it. In the end the idea was scrapped on the specious excuse that none of the British players had completed the entrance form properly. The only man who had got it right was the Canadian, George S. Lyon, who had won the first and last Olympic title for golf at St Louis in 1904. I must admit that it was new to me that golf had ever been an Olympic game, any more than cricket, which featured once, in 1900, when England beat the only other competitor – guess who? France! Our representatives then were the Devon County Wanderers who beat All Paris handsomely.

The Club began life as the St George's Golf Club in 1887 under the leadership of Dr Laidlaw Purves and fellow-members of Royal Wimbledon who were looking for a links course reasonably near London. It was essentially a London club in the early days, attracting professional men, lawyers, doctors, politicians, the City. The first President was Lord Granville, the Warden of the Cinque Ports, with the ten-year-old Lord Guilford as Vice-President, as the course was constructed on his land.

Notable in the Club's story is the service of three generations of Whitings as professional to the club, starting in 1911 when Fred Whiting, a noted club-maker, took over from Tom Vardon, the younger brother of the great Harry. A good example of Fred Whiting's power of repartee matches, I think, the famous 'Are we playing how or how many?' by the late Lloyd Mangrum. As the centenary handbook tells us, a sharp opponent, faced with a short but dubious putt to halve the match, said: 'I don't suppose you want to see me hole that one?'; to which Fred replied: 'No, but I'd like to see you try.'

As we have seen, the Club was soon in the Big Time, and in 1902 it applied for the royal title through its Member of Parliament, F. W. Fison. This was granted by King Edward VII via the Home Office as follows:

COPY of Prefix 'ROYAL' authorisation dated 17 May 1902

Any further communication on the subject of this letter should be addressed to:-
THE UNDER SECRETARY
OF STATE,
HOME OFFICE,
LONDON, S.W., WHITEHALL
and the following number quoted:-
B37,949/2.

17th May 1902

Sir,

I am directed by Mr Secretary Ritchie to acquaint you that he has had the honour to submit to The King the application of the Committee of the St. George's Golf Club, Sandwich, for permission to use the prefix 'Royal', and that His Majesty has been graciously pleased to comply with the Committee's wishes by commanding that the Club be styled 'The Royal Saint George's Golf Club'.

I am,
Sir,
Your obedient Servant,
[Signed Charles S. Murdoch]

F.W. Fison, Esq., M.P.,
64, Pont Street,
S.W.

ROYAL ASHDOWN FOREST

It is a tribute to the greatness of golf as a pastime that it can be enjoyed in surroundings as different as the linksland of Sandwich, the parkland of Mid-Surrey, the Downs of Eastbourne and the rough, tough moorland here at Forest Row. It is difficult to imagine four courses more unlike each other than these, and yet all provide excellent entertainment.

Without doubt Ashdown Forest has altered less with time than almost any course I can remember, with the possible exception of Brancaster. Here it is possible to feel and appreciate the game our fathers and grandfathers enjoyed, yet at the same time to have to play a good solid round to compete with its problems and its length.

This is a totally natural golf course without a single artificial bunker on the entire layout and, with one exception, no man-made hazards at all. Streams, heather, bracken, pits and hollows, humps and natural banks, some trees at the lower levels, severe slopes both up and down and some sandy roads, these are enough to use all the skill you possess without artificial additives. And surprisingly attractive all this is, especially as the upper holes give you such fine views over the Forest into the bargain.

Ashdown Forest has long been a stronghold of artisans' golf, and the Cantelupe Club for years produced a crop of famous players: many of the Mitchell family, including that superb striker of the ball, Abe Mitchell, who should have won the Open but never did, and Alfred Padgham, one of a large local family, who did win it in 1936. Many years ago I played much with Alf Padgham at Ashdown Forest when he was a young assistant and unknown. As a young slasher I was envious of his easy, lazy swing which made the game look so simple, and his quiet placid manner. Another famous character was Abe Mitchell's Aunt Polly, who caddied for forty years and kept a terse and splendidly human diary, so delightfully reported by Henry Longhurst.

The Duke of Cambridge (1819–1904) played his first golf shot at Royal Ashdown Forest in full military uniform

Famous too was John Rowe, the club's professional for fifty-five years, who was succeeded by Hector Padgham, who has been at the club nearly as long. There must be few clubs who have had only two professionals in a hundred years.

The Club was formed in 1887, and I am indebted to the club historian, Mr Henry Arnell, for giving me access to his findings on the grant of royal status to the Ashdown Forest and Tunbridge Wells Golf Club in 1893.

It all began when the Army held manoeuvres on Ashdown Forest in May of that year, under the command of the Duke of Cambridge, Queen Victoria's first cousin. The Duke, who in the few weeks that separated his birth from Victoria's in 1819 had been potentially heir to the throne, was an Army man all his life, commanding the Guards and Highland Division in the Crimea and ending as Commander in Chief of the Army.

Continuing now with Henry Arnell:

> During this period officers were accorded temporary membership of the Club, played golf and were given much hospitality. General Lord William Seymour, who commanded Dover, was on the Forest for the exercises, and being a golfing enthusiast played over the course. On 22nd May he was elected Field Marshal of the Club. This title appears to have originated at Royal Blackheath in the early days of the 19th century to distinguish an officer of the club who today we would call the President: his function was to 'marshal the field' when stroke play was first introduced. (Incidentally, the rank of Field Marshal in the British Army dates from 1736.)
>
> In mid-month HRH the Duke of Cambridge, C-in-C of the British Army, was pleased to write his name in the Members Book when he visited Forest Row to inspect the troops. One day Lord William persuaded the Duke to play his first ever golf shot, which he did from the first tee, having arrived there on horseback from his pitched tent on the Ladies' course. Attired in cocked hat with plumes, tight blue coat and a sword, he took a club from John Rowe, the Professional, who had made it specially for him, and played off. It was quite a good shot for his first attempt and travelled some 60 yards – the Duke was delighted!

As John Rowe recalled in an interview in a Sussex newspaper:

> [the Duke was delighted] and asked me to show him how I would drive. And in spite of some anxiety on my part that my own shot might be muffed, I drove a really good one and the 'Old Boy' was really pleased with it . . .
>
> The ball was retrieved again [explained Rowe] and there and then I wanted it kept and looked after. Its value as a souvenir of that historic moment was obvious. But there was a reverend gentleman whose eagerness and enthusiasm insisted that he too should drive the ball played by the Duke.
>
> The Rev. C. C. Woodland had the backing of the Committee; 'Oh let him have a shot John' they urged. And Tall John with justifiable misgiving, and on the promise that the shot would not go astray, placed the ball for him. It was a bad shot with the ball landing in the forest. Hours were spent in frustrating and painful search. An impossible task but hope was not abandoned until after several hours and night had descended.

As Arnell goes on:

> The President of the Club, Earl De La Warr, whose son Viscount Cantelupe was ADC to the Duke, knew him and Lord William Seymour and may well have been encouraged to apply for permission for the Club to use the title 'Royal'. In fact he did so, and received a letter from the Home Office dated 28th June 1893 giving permission which he forwarded to Mr. Birch, the Hon. Secretary.
>
> Letter from Earl De La Warr & Buckhurst, President of R.A.F.G.C. to Mr R. M. P. Birch, Hon. Secretary of R.A.F.G.C.

60 Grosvenor Street
29th June [1893]

Dear Mr. Birch,
I have the pleasure of enclosing the permission of Her Majesty to the Ashdown Forest Golf Club, to use the Title 'Royal'.
Yours faithfully
De La Warr & Buckhurst

Secretary of State
Home Department
B. 14654/2 WHITEHALL
28th June 1893

My Lord,
With reference to Your Lordship's letter of the 16th inst:, applying for permission to make use of the title 'Royal' in connection with the name of the Ashdown Forest and Tunbridge Wells Golf Club, I have the honour by direction of the Secretary of State to inform Your Lordship that he has laid the application before the Queen and that Her Majesty has been graciously pleased to accede to Your Lordship's request and to command that the Ashdown Forest and Tunbridge Wells Golf Club shall be called the 'Royal Ashdown Forest and Tunbridge Wells Golf Club'.
I have the honour to be,
My Lord,
Your Lordship's obedient Servant,
(Sgd) G. LEIGH PEMBERTON
The Right Honourable The Earl De-La-Warr,
60 Grosvenor Street, W.

The Ashdown Ladies' Club with its own course and club house, like the Sunningdale Ladies', was formed in 1889 and for years remained independent.

As Henry Arnell tells us:

Although it had always been assumed that the Ladies' Golf Club was entitled to be called 'Royal' because of their close association with the main Club, some doubt still existed. In order to seek clarification on this point advice was sought from the Home Office, and it was therefore with great pleasure that a letter was received from them dated 29th April 1932 confirming that official permission was granted for the club to be known as 'The Royal Ashdown Forest Ladies' Golf Club'.

Reference No:-
597,173
29th April, 1932

Madam,
I am directed by the Secretary of State to inform you that the application of the Ashdown Forest Ladies' Golf Club for permission to adopt the title 'Royal' has been laid before The King, and that His Majesty has been graciously pleased to Command that the Club shall henceforth be known as 'The Royal Ashdown Forest Ladies' Golf Club'.
I am,
Madam,
Your obedient Servant,
(Sgd) C. J. EAGLESTON
The Secretary,
Ashdown Forest Ladies' Golf Club,
Forest Row,
Sussex.

Arnell continues:

The new Ladies' course was unique in that it was not only the second of its kind in England to be especially designed for Ladies' golf but it was also the longest Ladies' course in the country and the only one to be Royal.* It was longer than Sunningdale Ladies' course and, according to the then ruling body, of championship length.

Unfortunately financial difficulties arose and the separate Ladies' Club was wound up in 1951 and their course passed into other hands.

ROYAL WINCHESTER

It is fitting that a city as famous as Winchester should have a royal golf club, even if the Club and course have had no great impact on the annals of the game.

* Not so, the Eastbourne Ladies' was also honoured.

Winchester has had a history as rich as that of any town in England. Identified as Camelot, it was the national capital before the Conquest, notably under King Alfred. It built its first cathedral in the seventh century, surpassed by the great Norman edifice of the eleventh century, which we see today, and it saw the foundation of William of Wykeham's famous school in 1378. The date fixed for the burial in the cathedral choir of its famous bishop, St Swithin, who died in the year 862, has given rise to the belief that rain on that day will spoil your golf holiday, if you have chosen late July or August for it. Another more tangible survival of Winchester's past is the continued provision from the Alms House of the Wayfarer's Dole of bread and beer to travellers in need.

In more modern times Winchester has been a garrison town associated with the proud Rifle regiments and now the headquarters of the Light Division. At my school we were permitted to use the Rifle Brigade's march 'I'm 95', to which some ribald words had been attached.*

The golf club here was started by the enthusiasm of the masters of the school, aided by the interest of officers from the barracks. Almost all the masters played, and I see among the list of names that of the Second Master, the father of my friend Richard Fort, the MP who died untimely in an accident in 1959.

Royal Winchester has the distinction of having had two famous professionals, first Andra Kirkaldy from St Andrews, old soldier and rough diamond, who did not like the job and left after a few months. It is perhaps not surprising that Kirkaldy's style did not fit the manners of the Winchester masters, but he finished his distinguished career as the professional to the Royal and Ancient Club.

* What would all the ladies say
When the 95th [or Harrow boys] have gone away
And they find themselves in the family way
And a hell of a doctor's bill to pay?

He was succeeded by the young J. H. Taylor, who joined the club in 1892 and stayed for four years, during which he won his first Open in 1894 at Sandwich, defending it successfully at St Andrews the next year. From Winchester, JH went on to further fame, ending his golfing life as the professional at Mid-Surrey.

The Winchester Golf Club started life in 1888 on downland on Morn Hill, moving to its present site on Teg Down in March 1901. In 1896 the Duke of Connaught was asked by the Club for his patronage and permission to use the prefix 'Royal'. The answer was apparently favourable, but the letter was lost. In 1912 the club found that they had been in error in using the royal prefix and wrote to ask that their mistake should be condoned and the true title granted. This had a happy ending, as the text of the letters exchanged shows:

Wylie Croft,
Winchester
23rd December, 1912

Sir,

Winchester Golf Club

I am asked by the Committee of this Club to make application that the Secretary of State will consider a request that this Club may be allowed to use the prefix 'Royal', with a view of advising His Majesty The King to grant it. The circumstances under which the application is made are as follows:

In or about the year 1896 at the time His Royal Highness The Duke of Connaught was commanding at Aldershot, a letter was written on behalf of the Committee by Major Leonard Russell, Rifle Brigade, asking whether His Royal Highness would honour the Club by becoming its Patron and allow it to use the prefix 'Royal', and a reply was received by Major Russell from the Duke's Equerry (Captain Yarde Buller) in the affirmative.

This letter was handed by him to the then Secretary of the Club, Major General Twemlow, and from that date up to the present time, about 17 years, the Club has always used the prefix 'Royal' under the belief that it was entitled to do so.

The letter received by Major Russell has been lost, and the Committee are unable to trace it. I enclose a statement from him setting forth the facts as they occurred.

It now appears that the Club has acted wrongly in using the prefix, but I am to ask the Secretary of State to accept the assurance that this has been done entirely under a misapprehension with no knowledge that any offence was being committed but with a bona fide belief that in consequence of the letter to which reference has been made the Club was entitled to do so. My Committee venture to hope that in the circumstances the Secretary of State will see fit to advise His Majesty to grant us the privilege of continuing to use the title and that we may not be deprived of what we have for so many years looked upon as a very great honour.

With regard to the position of the Club, it was established in the year 1888, the first Captain being The Right Honourable the Earl of Northesk. It consists of about 350 Members of whom about 85 are ladies, and the Committee venture to think that the Club may be said to be of good standing, the Members being drawn principally from the residents of the neighbourhood and Service Members stationed in the locality. In 1907 His Royal Highness Prince Arthur of Connaught did the Club the honour of joining it as an Honorary Member.

The financial position of the Club is perfectly sound.

For the information of the Secretary of State I beg to enclose the Rules and list of Members, also those of the Lady Members, from which will be gathered an idea of the constitution of the Club.

I also enclose the last Report of the Committee and the accounts for the past year.

If there is any other information which the Secretary of State requires it will be readily forthcoming and if he considers that I should attend to give any personal explanation I shall be most happy to do so. My Committee earnestly trust that this application may be favourably received.

I am Sir,
Your obedient Servant,
Hon. Sec.

Under Secretary of State
Home Office

Home Office,
Whitehall
2nd January, 1913

Sir,

With reference to previous correspondence, I am directed by the Secretary of State to inform you that His Majesty has been graciously pleased to approve of the Winchester Golf Club being allowed the privilege of using the prefix 'Royal', and to command that the Club be known as the 'Royal Winchester Golf Club'.

I am,
Sir,
Your obedient Servant,
(Sgd) A. J. EAGLESTON

Honorary Secretary,
Royal Winchester Golf Club,
Wyke Croft,
Winchester.

ROYAL BIRKDALE

Birkdale is big golf, big in every sense – the course, the Club, the atmosphere and the events which it has housed. All this has come to pass well on in Birkdale's history, for, although the Club is celebrating its centenary in 1989, it was not until 1946 that the first major event, the Amateur Championship, was held here (though, but for the War, it would have been host to the 1940 Open Championship). Since then honours have come in profusion: the Walker Cup in 1951, the Ryder Cup for the pros in 1965 and 1969 (which ended in a tie); the Open in 1954, 1961, 1965, in 1971 (the 100th), 1976 and 1983; and the Ladies' Open too in 1982 and 1986.

Royal Birkdale

Great play too has come with these events – the prodigious shot out of terrible rough by Arnold Palmer in his conquering prime, now commemorated by a plaque, the charge by the unknown Ballesteros, polite Mr Lu who almost won, the serene triumphs of Peter Thomson from Australia, who did; nine holes in '28 by an unknown journeyman pro called Durnian, Trevino taking seven at the 71st hole and still winning, Hale Irwin missing a two-inch putt and losing; and finally the nerveless brilliance of Tom Watson winning his fifth British Open in nine years.

Nowhere do the sandhills and the linksland more loudly declare that here is true seaside golf, and yet – and yet – the course somehow doesn't quite totally fulfil the promise of that first view. The fairways, which mostly run along the valleys and rarely cross the great dunes, lack the folds and ripples and the spare boniness of the old-style links, and the rough is fiercer than at, say, St Andrews or Rye. The result is a little too much lushness and flatness in the fairways and greens and too stern problems in the rough, what some American players have criticized as 'the Americanization of a links'. None the less, with strategic placing of the numerous bunkers, the shaping of the fairways and the excellent greens, Birkdale provides a strong test of golf and is a course well fitted to 'lie in the line of battle', with any in Britain. Peter Thomson, who had good reason to enjoy Birkdale, wrote:

> Birkdale lacks nothing. It is a man-size course but not a monster. It is testingly narrow but not absurd, and certainly not artificial. The turf is superb and its greens at their best have that superlative glassy smoothness that only championship venues provide. By every standard it is as modern as supersonic planes.

As the late Tom Scott, the Editor of *Golf Illustrated*, wrote: 'There is a curious belief in the minds of a few golfers that the Royal Birkdale is a comparatively new club.' It began, indeed, like so many golf clubs in England, by a few enthusiasts getting together under the leadership of one man, here Mr J. C. Barrett, and deciding to form a golf club. As usual, a modest 9-hole course was laid out, in 1889; then, as interest grew, came a move to better grounds and extension to 18 holes, this in 1897. Finally came reconstruction, a new layout and club house and – hey presto! – in 1931 here was a great potential championship links amid the great sandhills of Southport.

The royal title came along in due course, and the Club was informed officially of the honour by the Home Office in November 1951 – the last English club to be so distinguished! In all Britain only Royal Troon has been 'knighted' since.

ROYAL CINQUE PORTS, DEAL

This great course makes contact with its famous neighbour Royal St George's, but for all that offers you a different style of links

Arnold Palmer, who won the Open Championship at Royal Birkdale in 1961

golf, more open, closer to the sea – too close for comfort sometimes – tougher and possibly slightly less attractive, but as fine a test of golf as can be found, especially beating in against a south-west wind. Of all the four hundred courses I have played this is my favourite. I know no hole more superb, more calculated to raise one's game, than the great 16th, not to mention other splendid holes in the last five.

It was after playing at Deal that Lord Balfour, when he was plain mister, is reported to have said: 'The wit of man has never invented a pastime to equal golf.' Bernard Darwin wrote: 'Deal is a truly great course. I incline myself to think it the most testing and severe of all the championship courses.'

Cinque Ports has been ill-treated over its share of the Open Championships. It held its first in 1909, when J. H. Taylor won for the third time, and again in 1920, when George Duncan had a spectacular win over Abe Mitchell, who had been thirteen shots ahead at the half-way stage, all lost in one round. It

Royal Cinque Ports Club at Deal

would have hosted the 1915 Championship but for World War I, and the Championships of 1938 and 1949 if the sea had not broken in and wrecked the course. The sea broke in again in 1953 and 1978, and it was not until 1981 that a sea-wall was completed to ensure that this disaster would not recur. It is, however, arguable that the salt-water treatment, although damaging in the short term, has encouraged fine grasses, especially on the greens in the long.

It is unlikely that the Open will come back to Royal Cinque Ports; space would not be available for all the auxiliary activities of today; but the Amateur has been here twice, the last time in 1982.

Deal, I think, is most famous for the Halford–Hewitt competition, which is played by 640 golfers of 64 Public Schools Old Boys' Societies by foursomes each April.

The first professional here was Harry Hunter, who served the club from 1892 until 1935. He was the father of Willie Hunter, who won the Amateur Championship at Hoylake in 1921, put Bobby Jones out of the US Amateur in 1922, turned pro and prospered at the Riviera Club at Los Angeles. Here his son Mac Hunter succeeded him, to be succeeded in his turn at Riviera by his son.

The Deal Club was started in 1892 by local enthusiasts under the leadership of Major-General Graham, who became the first Captain. The Club was supported from the start by the town of Deal, which presented a fine Challenge Cup, and later trophies were given by successive Wardens of the Cinque Ports.

The Prince of Wales, later King George V, played here in 1910 and in September of that year, after he had become King, the Club asked for his patronage and the use of the royal title. The royal patronage was immediately granted, but not the title. The Club, however, in all innocence assumed otherwise. The unauthorized use of the title did not come to light for thirty-nine years, until 1949, when King George VI agreed to put matters right and the Royal Cinque Ports Golf Club was properly 'canonized'.

ROYAL MID-SURREY

If ever a club deserved a royal title, this one assuredly stands out. Located on Crown Land rich with historical associations with the Kings of England, Royal Mid-Surrey is deservedly famous, not only for past history but for its own conduct and reputation acquired since it began life almost a century ago.

Formed in 1892 by a local group of would-be players, the Club became sub-tenants of the farmer who leased the fields in Old Deer Park, Richmond, from the Crown. The Club, called 'Mid-Surrey' – not for its location but for its proximity to Middlesex, across the Thames – became the direct tenant of the land in 1894 and so remains. Since then the Club has prospered and grown prodigiously, has made the most of somewhat unpromising land, built two courses, cherished and encouraged ladies, young players and artisans and formed valuable reciprocal partnerships with important clubs all over the world. Famous professionals have served the club. In 1926–7 the Prince of Wales (later King Edward VIII) became Captain, and in 1926 his father, King George V, gave his consent to the grant of the royal title to the Club. In 1936 the new King became Patron of the Royal Mid-Surrey.

The royal associations with the Old Deer Park go back at least to King Henry V, who, just before leaving for the Agincourt campaign in 1415, founded the great Charterhouse of Sheen and a sister-foundation across the river at Sion, where alternate masses were sung for the repose of his soul. The traces of this great Carthusian monastery are buried under the fairways of the 14th and 15th holes of the main course.

A hundred years later Cardinal Wolsey spent a month after his disgrace at this monastery, before he died in 1530.

More recently George II used Richmond

Pam Barton with the United States and British Amateur Championship trophies at Royal Mid-Surrey

Lodge here as a retreat; so did George III, who directed Sir William Chambers to build the observatory building which stands in the heart of the golf-course today. Sir William Herschel, the astronomer to the Court, who discovered the planet Uranus in 1781, was its first director.

Next-door to Royal Mid-Surrey are Kew Gardens with their wonderful horticultural collection and a Chinese pagoda visible from the course. In the great gale of October 1987, the worst for over 250 years, Kew suffered appallingly; hundreds of priceless mature trees, many of them rare exotics, were blown down and lost. Some of Kew's broken trees spilled over on to the golf-course, which itself suffered comparatively little, with the grand 450-year-old cedar tree at the 12th hole surviving one more storm.

Famous names go with famous clubs, and first and most renowned at Mid-Surrey must surely be J. H. Taylor, five times Open Champion and four times runner-up, whom we have met already at Westward Ho! and Winchester. He was professional at Mid-Surrey from 1899 until 1946, when he was succeeded by Henry Cotton, three times Open winner.

Among amateurs famous at Royal Mid-Surrey we must assuredly go back to the early days and name S. H. (Stephen) Fry, not only a very fine golfer but also, and in a different class of excellence, a champion billiards player.

And then among lady golfers, not just of Royal Mid-Surrey but of all England, who can match the record of Pam Barton, who was both British and American Ladies' Champion in 1936 at the age of nineteen? No one, at least unless we go back to 1909 and Miss Dorothy Campbell, the Scot who won the British, American and Canadian Championships in her day, a feat only matched by Miss Marlene Streit, the Canadian. Pam Barton, who might have achieved many more triumphs at golf, was killed in a flying accident in 1943 as an officer in the RAF, aged twenty-six.

Now to the course itself. Frank Pennink, whose writing and judgement I admire, says this:

> It is a great example of what can be done on an almost entirely flat tract of ground . . . and it has embraced the fullest use of trees of which there are large numbers of most handsome specimens, with the placing of bunkers and the raising of greens above the surrounding level. It is a fine examination of golf.*

---

* Frank Pennink, *Choice of Golf Courses* (London: A. & C. Black, 1976).

CHAPTER 8

Wales, Ireland and the Islands

WALES

Although there are only two golf-courses in Wales with the royal title it can be said that what may be a lacking in quantity is more than made good by the quality, for the golf provided at Royal Porthcawl in the south, and Royal St David's at Harlech in the north is first class, as good as any in Britain.

Royal Porthcawl

The course here is located on the Welsh coast of the Bristol Channel, with fine views across to the hills of Devon and Exmoor and along to the Gower peninsula. Porthcawl can make the claim, rare indeed among seaside courses, that the sea is visible from every hole. The course has what is often regarded as the ideal layout, triangular in shape, thus giving as fair a test as possible when conditions are windy, as indeed they often are.

Porthcawl is a mixture of linksland, close to the shore, in places painfully close, and an upper level of almost moorland turf beset by bracken, heather and gorse in the rough. This gives a course of great variety, not abominably long at 6605 yards off the back tees; but with small greens, slopes and curves and a liberal supply of bunkers, it is by no means easy.

Porthcawl only joined the championship rota comparatively recently, being chosen for the Amateur in 1951, and again in 1965, 1973, 1980 and 1988. The first champion crowned here was Dick Chapman in an all-American final, while his fellow-countryman Dick Siderowf won in 1973. In 1965 it was the year for Michael Bonallack's second win out of five, and in 1980 in wind and storm Duncan Evans became the first Welshman to become Amateur Champion.

Royal Porthcawl has also had the distinction of being host to the Ladies' Championship, the Curtis Cup contest against the ladies of the USA and the Amateur Home Internationals.

The Club was founded in 1891, when play was organized with 9 holes on a piece of land called Lock's Common. This did not suffice for long, and the Club moved to the present excellent site in 1898. The layout it seems has altered comparatively little, apart from some changes by Harry Colt in 1913, by Tom Simpson in 1933 and by C. K. Cotton in 1950. J. V. Moody gives a splendid description of the start of affairs at Porthcawl:

> H. J. Simpson, the club's first captain, can probably lay claim to being the real founder ably backed-up by the Vivian brothers, Willie and Harry, who were deputised to attend a vestry meeting at the old Lamb and Flag to apply for the consent of the parish vestry to play Golf on Lock's Common.
>
> No-one in the room other than the two brothers knew anything at all of the game and the vestry – probably a sort of council despite its religious connotations – was told that there would be nine holes, so many hundred feet apart in a zig-zag fashion, and that the holes would be about four or five inches in diameter and depth.
>
> A vestry man asked with astonishment 'Is that all?'

Mr Vivian . . . 'Yes, sir.'

'Well,' said the pleased vestry man, 'I do now move that the consent of the vestry be given to Messrs Harry and W. S. Vivian to cut the turf as suggested by them for the playing of the game known as golf.'

'I second' said another and the motion was carried.

The brothers, after thanking the vestry men for their consent, deposited half-a-crown on the table. As soon as the sound of their footsteps had died away one vestry man said 'I move now we have a jug in.' This was duly carried; the jug was brought in and sent around.

Business continued and then another request for a drink round, and all partook of the contents of the jug. Obviously it was not the last because sometime during the evening a song was composed entitled 'Who sold the Lock's Common for a gallon of drink.' There was never a vestry again in a public house.

On 30 March 1909 the Club was granted the rare privilege to use the prefix 'Royal'.

On 1 April 1909 the *South Wales Daily News* printed a short paragraph under the heading 'ROYAL PORTHCAWL':

> The Lord Mayor of Cardiff received the intimation that it was the intention of His Majesty to confer the title Royal on the Porthcawl Golf Club. This is the result of efforts which have been made for months past by Mr Wyndham Jenkins, Captain of the Club, to secure Royal recognition of the institution.

At that time there were twenty-one Royal golf clubs in existence, with the Royal St David's Club at Harlech the only one in Wales. There followed the text of the official letter to the Lord Mayor:

> My Lord . . . With reference to your letter of 30 November last I am directed by the Secretary of State to inform you that he has had the honour to submit to the King for His Majesty's favourable consideration the application of the Porthcawl Golf Club to be permitted to use the prefix Royal and that His Majesty has been graciously pleased to command that the Club be henceforth known as the Royal Porthcawl Golf Club – I am My Lord, Your obedient servant.

According to Sq. Ldr Samuel, the Secretary of the Club, whose help we gratefully acknowledge:

> There is no precise record of how this was achieved. Certain moves had been made earlier, but the first response from the Home Secretary was far from encouraging: '. . . respecting the petition of the Porthcawl Golf Club for permission to use the title Royal, I am sorry to have to inform you that this petition has been submitted to the King but having regard to the precedents which govern such grants, after careful consideration I was unable to advise His Majesty to grant the desired privilege'. The Home Secretary was Herbert Gladstone, the youngest son of W E Gladstone, four times Liberal Prime Minister. Herbert Asquith was Liberal Prime Minister in 1908. The correspondence was addressed to Sidney Robinson, Liberal Member for Brecon and Radnor, a Vice-President of the club and Captain in 1903.
>
> It must be a matter of conjecture as to what transpired between the formal rejection and the receipt of another letter just six months later dated 30 March 1909: '. . . referring to our previous correspondence about the Porthcawl Golf Club, I am glad to inform you that after enquiry and consideration I have felt able to recommend the King to permit the Club to use the title "Royal" and that His Majesty has been pleased to approve the recommendation. Signed H E Gladstone.'

Royal St David's, Harlech

This course has as fine a situation as any in the world, as good I would say as that enjoyed by Royal County Down, Pebble Beach or Banff Springs in western Canada. Down on the linksland below the little town

A view of the first hole at Royal Porthcawl

of Harlech the golfers can look up with pride and joy to the great, overbearing castle of King Edward I, built in 1299, towering over all other man-made efforts, with the backdrop of the mountains of the Snowdon range to the north to make a majestic addition to the picture. Edward I built the castle after he had conquered Wales. Afterwards he proclaimed his son Prince of Wales, which may or may not have reconciled the Welsh to his conquest, but at least two of the Prince's descendants became, respectively, a Patron and a Captain of the Club. The castle was the last stronghold of King Charles I to fall to Cromwell in the Civil War.

Scenery apart, I think that the Harlech Club must yield the first prize for Welsh golf to Porthcawl: the course is not quite so excellent and the importance of the events held there not quite so great. The layout, as is so often found at links courses, has a mixture of flat, mildly lumpy, difficult holes and of others with great sandhills embracing insinuating fairways and greens in dells or plateaux. At Harlech the proportion, I felt, was rather too much weighted in favour of the flat holes against one's full seaside expectations.

The Ladies' Championship has been held here four times, and like all great courses Harlech has produced some worthy winners. Notable perhaps is the win of the American girl Barbara McIntyre, in that not once in the entire tournament, I believe, did she take three putts.

The Club was founded in 1894, and in the words of the club handbook:

> Soon after its inception Edward VII, then Prince of Wales, became a patron of the Club,

The thirteenth-century castle of Harlech of Edward I forms the backdrop to the 18th green at Royal St David's

whereupon the overkeen members proudly and promptly assumed the prefix 'Royal'. This slight faux-pas was righted when eleven years later the King sanctioned the present title of the Royal St David's Golf Club. The Duke of Windsor, when Prince of Wales, was Captain of the Club in 1935 and came down specially to play himself in.

The letter putting right the error made in 1901 over the royal title read as follows:

From The Under Secretary of State
Home Office
London S.W.

WHITEHALL
15 August 1908

Sir
I am directed by Mr. Secretary Gladstone to acquaint you that the application of the St. David's Golf Club to be allowed to use the prefix 'Royal' has been graciously acceded to by His Majesty, who has signified His Pleasure that the Club should be known as the Royal St. David's Golf Club, Harlech. The Secretary of State regrets that the Club should have wrongfully adopted the prefix in 1901.

I am,
Sir,
Your obedient Servant
Henry Cunningham

IRELAND

As part of the United Kingdom in the nineteenth century, Ireland was garrisoned by British troops, and it was they that brought golf to Ireland in the 1850s, so beginning the process which has led to the building of golf-courses as fine, if not finer, than any in the British Isles or indeed anywhere in the world. And a fine crop of golfers has come from Ireland too.

Organized golf began here in 1881 in Belfast, followed soon afterwards by clubs in the south. The clubs in Ireland with the royal title, in order of date of formation, are these:

1	Royal Belfast	1881
2	(Royal) Curragh	1883
3	Royal Dublin	1885
4	Royal Portrush	1888
5	Royal County Down	1889

Royal Belfast

Now well past its centenary, Royal Belfast has had an uneventful history following the usual pattern, from small beginnings to rapid flowering, enlargement, changes of venue, wartime anxieties and now a rich, ripe maturity secured by a large and congenial membership and no doubt a substantial waiting list.

The speed of progress here at the start, as often elsewhere, astounds one today. The founders of the Club, Thomas Sinclair and George Baillie, who had learned golf in Scotland, met to discuss the project in October 1881; on 5 November a circular went out, calling a meeting to be held in the Chamber of Commerce on 9 November presided over by the Mayor of Belfast. Seven weeks later, on Boxing Day, the first competition was held on the newly built course on the Kinnegar at Hollywood. The best scores on that day were 121, 130 and 131 for 18 holes. Dr Collier, head of the Royal Academy, had a net 200 and the last score in was 228.

The course at the Kinnegar was originally of 6 holes, then of 9. By 1892 overcrowding brought about a move to another seaside site at Carnalea, where, it was said, 'Its existence was placid. It took little part in more public aspects of the game.' By 1925 public incursions made Carnalea unattractive, and the club bought the fine mansion it now occupies in Craigavad, also on that deep arm of the sea called Belfast Lough, a really fine site. Here an excellent water-side 18-hole course was laid out by H. S. Colt.

The Belfast Club has enjoyed royal patronage singe 1885, when the Prince of Wales was on a visit to Ireland. The President, Captain Harrison, secured this distinction, and a letter from the Private Secretary of the Prince from Marlborough House dated 30 June 1885 conferred the honour. The royal patronage was held to confer also the royal title. This is confirmed by a letter from the Keeper of the Privy Purse in 1901 stating that King Edward VII would continue his patronage of the *Royal* Belfast Golf Club. Subsequently George V and George VI became Patrons, and later the Duke of Edinburgh accepted the title.

(Royal) Curragh

In 1855, at the time of the Crimean War, large Army camps were constructed at Aldershot, at Shorncliff and at The Curragh, the last on a wide stretch of heathland in County Kildare about 30 miles from Dublin. This was a major undertaking, as the camp was designed to house 10,000 troops.

The Curragh Golf Club was created by initiative of the officers of Scottish regiments based at the camp in 1883, which makes it one of the oldest clubs in Ireland. For all that, golf was played on this site as early as the 1850s, in an area known as Donnelly's Hollow, and there are records of a match there in 1852. Donnelly, by the way, was a bare-knuckle prize-fighter who won a famous victory here in 1815. His right arm is apparently preserved at the Hideout Public House in Kilcullen.

Military necessity caused frequent changes to the golf layout, and the Club suffered severely when the camp was almost emptied of troops in 1899 by the South African War and again in 1914 by the Kaiser's War.

The post-war troubles and struggles for Irish independence also made difficulties, but all was settled, or so it was thought, by the Treaty of 1921, by which Ireland was partitioned and the twenty-six counties of the south and west formed the independent Irish Free State. On 16 May 1922, in the pouring rain, the last British troops marched out of the Curragh camp, and the army of Eire took over. Apparently the departing British took with them the club records and also sold the golf pavilion, which left things rather bare.

On 6 August 1910 the Commander in Chief of the Forces in Ireland, Major-General Lyttelton, wrote to the Secretary of State at the Home Office in these terms:

> Sir: I have the honour to request that you will be good enough to ascertain from the King whether His Majesty would be graciously pleased to grant The Curragh Golf Club the honour of His patronage and to authorise it to assume the prefix 'Royal'.
>
> It has been impossible to ascertain definitely by whom, or how, the Club was formed, the old Minute Books having unfortunately been lost about the time of the South African War, but the 'Irish Golfers' Guide' states that the Club was formed about 1855, adding that 'the presence of Highland Regiments naturally led to golf-playing many years ago, and there is little doubt that the Curragh Golf Club is the oldest in Ireland' . . . I would add that the majority of the Committee and players consist of Officers of His Majesty's forces, and that all the members of the Club would deem it the greatest honour were it His Majesty's pleasure to confer such distinction on the Curragh Golf Club.

The title 'Royal' was conferred in a letter from the Home Office dated 24 September 1910, which was acknowledged by the Captain of the Club, Major-General Campbell, on 1 October.

When the Free State came into being there is no record that the royal title was repudiated; the first annual meeting in 1923 merely records that the Club should be called 'The Curragh Golf Club'. And so things stood for nearly sixty years, until Commandant Gibson, the Club's historian and Captain in 1985, enquired of the Privy Purse Office at Buckingham Palace how the royal grant stood. The Home Office – Mr L. P. Little – replied: 'We have no evidence to show that the title was ever withdrawn from the Club.' So the royal title is still valid, and, as Commandant Gibson, on UN duty in Lebanon, wrote, 'ranks the club in a very select group'.

While the (Royal) Curragh Golf Club has the distinction of having the title but not using it, the *Royal Tara Golf Club* awarded itself the title by virtue of its proximity to the Hill of Tara where the ancient Kings of Ireland used to dwell. It has no Royal Charter. To which information the Secretary, Mr Desmond Foley, has added: 'I am sure, therefore, that you will not require any further information in relation to Royal Tara'; and, on the whole, I am inclined to agree with him. While to style oneself 'Royal' in the UK would probably not be illegal, it would to say the least be a gross and unforgiveable breach of good manners. In a foreign country the word, being part of the English language, is not sacred, and no doubt if the Bellinter Park Club of Navan, County Meath, prospers as Royal Tara, others, perhaps in the USA (who knows?) might follow suit.

Royal Dublin

We now come to a club of the first rank, Royal Dublin, founded in 1886 by a small group of friends led by a Scot, Mr John Lumsden, who got a club started for organized play in Phoenix Park, Dublin. Golf had been played there before by officers from the British garrison, and they became enthusiastic supporters of the Dublin Golf Club.

An early member was Mr Balfour, later to be Prime Minister and later still an Earl, who was then Chief Secretary for Ireland. As he was a very prominent figure in English society, Balfour's love of golf did much to encourage the game south of the border. He joined the Dublin Club in 1887 and always played with two armed detectives in attendance who acted as caddies. Without doubt Balfour's support was invaluable in obtaining the royal title for the club. It was he who informed his fellow-members on 22 May 1891 that Her Majesty Queen Victoria had approved the change of name. Unfortunately the records were lost in the fire which destroyed the club house in August 1943.

The Dublin Club soon left Phoenix Park, and after a brief stay at Sutton moved to a splendid new seaside site on Bull's Island inside the city limits in 1889. Here, on a piece of recent and still growing sandy linksland, fed by the sea, an excellent layout was made. This, however, was wrecked by the takeover of the Island in 1914 by the military. So after World War I a fresh start was made, and the fine course of today, always known as Dollymount, was laid out by H. S. Colt, then the leading British designer, and has stood the test of time.

Quoting my own words from *Play the Best Courses*:

> The links is of the true metal, the ground though rather flat and without mountains of sand is of the proper sandy soil and the rough 'up to test' . . . Christy O'Connor once finished the round eagle, birdie, eagle but few of us can hope to follow that. Carrolls Irish Open has been played here with two wins for Ballesteros and one for Langer the German.
>
> Dollymount is a bird sanctuary and 3000 specimens have been identified there I was told but what I liked were the hares, big ones, young ones, little ones hopping about on their long legs or stopping with their big ears cocked to look and listen. They are fairly tame and unafraid as no guns are allowed on the Island. I startled a young one in the rough with its ears back; it sprang up from under my feet and ran off and you could see the little nest its body had made in the grass.

In 1962 the Club enquired of the Lord Chamberlain's Office whether a charter granting royal status could be found. The Home Office in reply stated that the royal title was indeed granted in 1891 but, in accordance with usual practice, simply by letter and that no formal charter existed. Mr Jauncey, who has been successively a Committee Member, Captain, Hon. Secretary and life member and trustee of Royal Dublin, who took so much trouble to help this book with details, staunchly tells us. 'No, there never has been in my 43 years of membership of the Club any question of the Club abandoning its "Royal Title".'

Royal Portrush

Up in the far north of Ireland, in County Antrim, is Portrush, once a small fishing village, now a successful holiday resort. On the coast here is one of the finest golf links in the world, H. S. Colt's masterpiece, laid out in stupendous tumbling dune country at the end of the twenties. Add to this splendid scenery, from the Giant's Causeway and the Skerries close in shore to the distant shapes of the Outer Isles of Scotland across the sea and the far distant hills of Donegal, and you have a wonderful place to play golf in, one of many wonderful and beautiful places to play golf in Ireland.

The Club was a hundred years old in 1988 and in its lifetime has seen many changes: the course now virtually a new one, a differently located club house and a less powerful but good second course further inland.

The Open was played here in 1951, Max Faulkner getting home with an average of just over 71 per round. The course held the upper hand all the way that year, and only two rounds in the whole tournament beat 70. The Amateur Championship was here in 1960 and gave forth an Irish victory, as Joe Carr beat Cochran, the American, in the final. In 1988, the centenary year, the Irish Close Championship was held here. Of men players from Portrush, first among the professionals is Fred Daly, who won the Open in 1947 and the British Match Play Championship in 1947, 1948 and 1952. Among the amateurs Lionel Munn was consistently and conspicuously the leader before and after World War I; later Noel Martin and Charles Hezlet played in the Walker Cup teams, and Hezlet was runner-up in the Amateur in 1914. The Hezlet sisters were even more distinguished. May Hezlet and Rhona Adair won the Ladies' Championship for Portrush five times in nine years, and the other two Hezlet girls were nearly as good, one or other being a Championship runner-up for years.

This is not the place for a course description, but two holes at Portrush command attention. The first of these is the 5th, of which I have written:

> you are on the tee, and there, surely much more than 392 yards away and below you, is the green on the edge of the Atlantic, with nothing but a sea of rolling dunes, rough and sandhills in between. Well, it's not as far as it looks and there is a fairway down there, so if you are not hypnotized by the scenery and don't try to cut off too much you can play it as a dog-leg and a very fair and reasonable hole it becomes . . . Then comes the 206-yard 'Calamity' fourteenth, an appalling narrow shot with utter disaster down a violent slope into a dell on the right and below the green and no help from the bumpy hillocks all along the hole on the left.

The Club handbook tells us:

> When the club was formed in May 1888, it was known as the County Club. It became the Royal County Club in 1892, when H.R.H. The Duke of York was its patron and the name was changed to 'The Royal Portrush Golf Club' in 1895, with H.R.H. The Prince of Wales (later King Edward VII) as patron.

Royal County Down, Newcastle

Here is another stupendously beautiful Irish course, 30 miles south of Belfast on the coast of County Down, under the shadow of the Mountains of Mourne, headed by Slieve Donard, 2800 feet high. Slieve Donard dominates the scene; now purple in the autumn light, now indigo, now dark bottle-green, now half hidden in mist and rainstorm, now glittering with rocks wet after rain has gone by, it is a perpetual joy.

Not only is this a wonderfully attractive course scenically, it is also just about the best and toughest golf links in the British Isles, admirably laid out in two separate and different 9s, each hole on its own, fair, just and *enjoyable*. Along with Deal and Sandwich, Newcastle is my favourite links, and I wish I could stand once more at the top of the hill looking down the fairway at the 9th to the plateau green and the mountains beyond.

Here is how things began in the clear story in the Club's handbook:

> It was almost a hundred years ago that today's famous course of the Royal County Down Golf Club at Newcastle, County Down, was conceived. In 1889 a Golf Club to be known as 'The County Down Golf Club' was formed and at a meeting in June of that year the minutes show that 'the Secretaries are empowered to employ Tom Morris to lay out the course at a cost not to exceed £4 (four pounds)'. Heaven knows how the good Tom utilised that sum for the course had to be cut out of rough ground and sand-hills. That success was achieved is beyond question for only four years later the first of the many championships which it has seen was played at Newcastle. And in 1898 in the book 'The World of Golf' it was written of Newcastle, 'the links are undoubtedly the finest in Ireland. I doubt indeed, if there are any superior in the world. The hazards are in some places rather startling to weak-kneed players, but the putting greens are things of beauty.'
>
> There were, naturally enough, various al-

Simone Thion de la Chaume of France, winner of the British Amateur title at Royal County Down in 1927

Simone Thion de la Chaume is pictured before her marriage to René Lacoste, winner of the singles tennis title at Wimbledon in 1925 and 1928

terations to those links at the end of last century, chief among these being a reconstruction which was completed in 1908. It was Harry Vardon writing of this reconstructed course who said: '. . . I have always thought Newcastle the best golf course in Ireland, and now it holds its own with all others'.

It was, too, in 1908 that His Majesty King Edward VII was graciously pleased to command that the prefix 'Royal' be added in perpetuity to the name of the Club, and that the Club be known in future by the title 'Royal County Down Golf Club'. A further Royal honour was bestowed in 1953 when His Royal Highness The Prince Philip, Duke of Edinburgh, became the Club's Patron.

The remoteness of Newcastle and the lack of space and facilities for an Open Championship have limited the use of this great course to the Amateur, which first came here in 1970 when Michael Bonallack showed his mastery by winning his fifth Championship, a feat second only to John Ball's eight wins.

The Ladies' Championship has been here seven times, and Newcastle has been a happy hunting-ground for French girls, Mlle Simone Thion de la Chaume winning here in 1927, the Vicomtesse de Saint Sauveur in 1950 and Mlle Varangot with the first of her three championships in 1963. Why French girls should be so good and French men so inconspicuous is one of golf's mysteries. In addition to what they did at Newcastle, Mlle Varangot won the British Ladies' Championship twice more, Mlle LeBlan once and Mlle Thion de la Chaume's daughter Cather-

Catherine Lacoste, their daughter, who won the British Amateur title in 1969 at Royal Portrush

Another French winner of the title at Royal County Down, Miss B. Varangot, in 1963

Madame Simone Lacoste, pictured in a match with Enid Wilson (left), Lady Heathcoat-Amory (Joyce Wethered) and Henry Cotton

Vicomtesse de Saint Sauveur, who won the British Amateur Championship at Royal County Down in 1950, is congratulated by the runner-up, Jessie Valentine of Scotland (left)

ine Lacoste won it at Portrush in 1969 and the US Ladies' in the same year. Not content with that, the prodigious Mlle Lacoste, daughter of a tennis champion and a golf champion, won the US Ladies' Open in 1967, against all the pros, a feat matched in 1987 by our Laura Davies.

THE ISLANDS

Unhappily my hope that we could perhaps have taken the ferry across to the Isle of Wight to play a round at Bembridge on the little 9-hole links which once was the home of the Royal Isle of Wight Golf Club failed, as the little links has been abandoned since 1961 in spite of a venerable history. As the Club's original handbook tells us, the story of the start is this:

The Royal Isle of Wight Golf Club can be said to have originated at a luncheon party held at the Royal Spithead Hotel in the spring of 1882, when to the assembled company that popular sportsman, Captain Jack Eaton, R.N., suddenly proposed the conundrum: 'What was the Duver meant for?'

The party hazarded various suggestions, but Jack Eaton would accept none of them, crying himself instead, 'It was made on purpose for Golf, and if you come over there I'll show you!' So across the harbour the party went and had explained to them the intricacies of a game which was at that time unknown in England, save to a few enthusiasts who played at Blackheath, Wimbledon and Westward Ho!

The course occupied a very small area near the village of St Helen's, protected from the sea by the sea-wall called the Duver, on which now repose some of the old coaches of the Isle of Wight Railway. The 9 holes wove in and out amongst themselves and gave you some fine shots among the dunes on the seaward side. On the beach here Mr Horace Hutchinson many years ago reported finding his ball lying upon 'a dead and derelict dog'. Continuing with the old handbook:

> The honour of driving the first ball fell to Mrs. Hambrough, wife of the Club's first captain, Dudley A. Hambrough, and she acquitted herself well in what must have been something of a trying ordeal. In strict truthfulness it must be recorded that at the first match the interest of many spectators was directed not so much at the players as at one of the caddies, who was a very pretty barmaid from the Royal Spithead Hotel! . . .
>
> On September 18th, 1883, a letter was received from the Secretary of State intimating that he had 'had the honour to submit to the Queen your [the Secretary's] request that the Isle of Wight Golf Club may be permitted to assume the title of "Royal", and that Her Majesty has been graciously pleased to accede to your request and to command that the Club be styled the "Royal Isle of Wight Golf Club" '.

King Edward VII and King George V became Patrons, and Prince Henry of Battenberg – father of Lord Mountbatten of Burma – was Captain of the Club in 1894–5. Many distinguished persons used to come to Bembridge, including Arthur Balfour and his two detectives. I am glad to be able to say that I have played it a time or two and remember now, nearly sixty years on, hitting a fine two-iron to the heart of the 'Punch Bowl' green with a putt for two. Halcyon days.

Alas, fashions changed. The family holidays in large hotels by the English seashore, like Winston Churchill's at Cromer in July 1914 when the World Crisis was approaching, did not long survive the War, and resorts like Bembridge and its Spithead Hotel went through a major change of life. The people that supported golf flocked abroad and the little Royal Isle of Wight Club could not keep up. In the end there were only a dozen members; the trophies and honours board went down to the Sandown & Shanklin Club and the land was given over to picnickers and the exercising of dogs. And yet – and yet – it could all come back, I think: the course could be recovered; and, looking at other titles, it seems not impossible that it could even be revived as the Royal Isle of Wight Golf Club.

So we should now move on to livelier royal courses in the Channel Islands, as the Isle of Man, though it has good golf, doesn't possess a Royal.

Royal Jersey

Founded in 1878, this is one of the oldest golf clubs outside Scotland. The Founding Fathers were Mr F. W. Brewster and seven friends aided and abetted by the officers of the Militia.

A course was developed on seaside turf on common land close to the shore of Grouville Bay on the eastern coast of the Island, with a fine view of the great Mont Orgueil Castle to the north. For over sixty years the peaceful pursuit of the game continued here and then in 1940 was violently overthrown by the appalling interruption of the German occupation of Jersey.

Although the behaviour of the enemy in the Channel Islands was less abominable than in many other places, the five years of occupation and rigid control were hard to bear, and the golf links of the Royal Jersey Club was among the casualties of these years. A little golf was still allowed until 1943, but by the end of the War the course was virtually obliterated. Trenches, gunpits, concrete blockhouses and emplacements, piles of gravel – one of them of half a million tons – light railways, mines in thousands and

PROCLAMATION

Certain incidents have occurred in which, on the part of the inhabitants of the Island, acts have been committed which were against the safety of the Army of Occupation. Those who were guilty have been, or will be, punished according to the decree of Martial Law by Sentence of Death.

In their own interest I warn the Public most solemnly against perpetrating any further acts of this kind. Any person involved in such an act, either as Perpetrator, Participant or Instigator will, upon conviction by Court Martial, without power of Appeal be condemned to suffer the Death Penalty.

In view of the present economic situation the recent Prohibition in regard to Fishing has been modified. If, however, this act of leniency is misunderstood, and certain individual and irresponsible elements of the population perpetrate further acts which are detrimental to the safety of the Army of Occupation, the entire population will have to suffer the consequences of the reprisals which will follow.

People of the Island! Your destiny and your welfare is in your own hands. Your Home Interests demand that you should refrain from and to the best of your power prevent, all such actions which must inevitably be followed by such disastrous consequences.

The Military Commander in France,
(Signed) v. STÜLPNAGEL,
General of Infantry.

Golf courses on the island of Jersey suffered under the occupation of the German forces during the Second World War when the residents often witnessed warning proclamation notices

a barbed wire jungle were imposed on this area by a horde of slave workers imported by the Master Race, and the water supply to the greens was put to other uses. And, in the end, it was the invaders that were made captive, hemmed in by the Allied landings in Normandy in 1944, and German prisoners who cleared up much of the mess which they had made. Even so the final restoration of the course after the prisoners had departed was still a major task, not easily comprehended today when we look on this green and pleasant, compact, attractive golf course on its piece of linksland. Few clubs other than its neighbour in Guernsey and Princes, Sandwich, its wounds inflicted by its defenders, have endured so much and survived.

We were proud to learn from the Captain, Mr Clive Dobin, that his father had succeeded in concealing from the enemy all the Club's records and trophies behind a false wall which he improvised and built in the club house; he also rescued the clubs and gear from the members' lockers and hid them safely in a warehouse in another part of the Island.

The Jersey Golf Club was quick off the mark in seeking royal favour. The Secretary, Mr Reg Waymouth, was kind enough to produce the original minute book of 1878, which records that at the first annual meeting of the club on 13 December 1878 it was 'unanimously resolved that application to obtain for the club the title *Royal* should be made by the Captain to the proper quarter'.

The application was made to the Lieutenant-Governor of Jersey, who forwarded it to the Home Secretary in London. On 22 January 1879 the Permanent Secretary at the Home Office, Godfrey Lushington, replied to the Lieutenant-Governor in these terms:

> Sir, I am directed to inform you with reference to your letter of the 7th instant, that Mr Secretary Cross has had the honour to submit to Her Majesty your request that the Jersey Golf Club may be permitted to assume the title of 'Royal' and that Her Majesty has been graciously pleased to accede to the request and to command that the Society in question shall be styled the 'Royal Jersey Golf Club'. I am Sir – your obedient servant (signed Godfrey Lushington).

The royal title was confirmed in subsequent reigns, as witnessed by documents preserved from German interference by Mr Dobin – from Whitehall to Government House in 1903 and from the Privy Purse Office in Buckingham Palace to the Captain of the Club in 1936.

A print of golf at Royal Jersey before the turn of the century

The Royal Jersey Club is unique, I think, in that its centenary was commemorated by the issue of a set of postage stamps.

The fame of the Channel Islands, Jersey especially, as the cradle of great golfers is so remarkable as to deserve, I think, a separate section, so we will leave Jersey with the note that on the Royal Jersey links at the 13th hole a stone has been erected bearing the words 'Within putting distance of this stone Harry Vardon (1870–1937) the great golfer was born; six times Open Champion 1896–98–99, 1903–11–14': a fitting memorial, simple and modest like the man it commemorates, to Britain's greatest player.

Royal Guernsey

Eighteen miles from Jersey, or twelve minutes by the local air service, is Guernsey, another, and in many ways quite different island, though enjoying similar independence from the United Kingdom. Guernsey has overlordship over the other islands of Alderney, Sark, Herm and Jethou.

The golf club is at the northern extremity of the Island on L'Ancresse Common, where the commoners have and exercise the right of public access and the grazing of animals. None the less, a fine golf-course has been fashioned out of the linksland and gorse-clad cliff slopes, by the renowned Scottish architect Mackenzie Ross, of Dornoch and Pinehurst fame, replacing the ravages to the old links by the 'Gentle Hun', as locally named, during the occupation. One of the invaders' feats was to dump all the Secretary's records out of the window and set fire to them, after which the club house was stripped and gutted down to a bare shell without even the floors surviving. The result of this

The Royal Guernsey course – Henry Cotton was a visitor to the island in his childhood

has been the almost complete lack of club records to add to the problems of reconstruction after the War of the entire terrain from its function as part of Hitler's Western Wall. Only the intervention of the States Government saved the club from going under from the damage caused by the occupation.

The Guernsey Club dates from 1890, with thirty-seven Founder Members, and within twelve months of its beginning it had applied through the Lieutenant-Governor for royal status. The Secretary, Mr Nicholle, was good enough to produce for us what records there are. These show that on 10 June 1891 the Secretary of the Lieutenant-Governor wrote to the Captain of the Club in these terms:

> Sir, I have the honour by direction of the Lieutenant-Governor to inform you agreeably of intimation from the Home Department that Her Majesty has been graciously pleased to comply with the humble request of the members of the Guernsey Golf Club that this association might be styled 'Royal' and has commanded that for the future the association shall be styled 'The Royal Guernsey Golf Club': I have the honour to be Sir, your obedient servant (signature . . . Bale).

This was accompanied by a letter from Godfrey Lushington of the Home Office Staff dated 2 June 1891, conveying the information to the Government Office in Guernsey. These documents grace the Club today, together with an engraving of Queen Victoria commemorating her Diamond Jubilee in 1897.

The Channel Island Golfers

The Channel Islands are survivors of the original Dukedom of Normandy brought to the British Isles in 1066. To this day, the Queen is properly known and addressed here as the Duke of Normandy, and her son will in his turn be the Duke.

Strongly loyal to the Crown but not part of the United Kingdom, the Islands have led a separate existence for over nine hundred years, with their own laws, customs and to a limited extent language, closer to the coast of France than to their homeland.

It is a strange fact that in the history of sport relatively small populations have from time to time produced a disproportionate number of great players, such as the scores of Australian Lawn Tennis champions after World War II. The Channel Islands and Jersey in particular have over the last hundred years produced a surprising number of good professional golfers and some of unquestionable championship ability.

From Guernsey came the Jolly brothers, of whom the best, Herbert, became a fine tournament player, and a member of the Ryder Cup team. Henry Cotton's mother came from Guernsey, and young Henry was a visitor here in childhood.

From Jersey came numerous Gaudins, Renoufs and Le Chevalliers, who made the grade as professionals, and from the La Moye end of the Island, Aubrey and Percy Boomer. Aubrey Boomer was a most successful competitor in the 1920s and a Ryder Cup man, while Percy wrote a famous book of instruction.

In earlier times there was a genial giant, Ted Ray, whose 'boisterous good humour and slashing play' Bobby Jones enjoyed. Ray, like Vardon, was born near the Royal Jersey links. He won the British Open in 1912 and in 1913 tied for first in the US Open, to be beaten in the play-off by young Francis Ouimet. In 1920 at Inverness, Ohio, he won the US Open, beating his fellow-Jerseyman and friend Harry Vardon, who should have won, by one stroke.

It is said that Ray, who always smoked a pipe when playing, when he heard that he had a putt of 3 feet 6 inches to win, stepped back, relit his pipe, took a couple of draws and, with the smoke going nicely, banged the ball into the hole.

So we come to Harry Vardon, the son of a gardener, born in a small cottage on the links of the Club at Grouville, with a passing glance at his younger brother Tom, who was also a fine golfer.

Harry was, I think, unquestionably the finest player Britain has produced. He won the Open six times, a feat which has so far eluded the super-golfers of today. He won the US Open once, in 1900, tied for first in 1913 with Ouimet and Ray, losing the play-off, and was second in 1920 in his three attempts. He set new standards of accuracy, and, as Bernard Darwin said, 'he raised the whole standard of the game which others felt driven to emulate'. Herbert Warren Wind, the American writer of distinction, calls him 'the first modern golfer'. His smooth, economical upright swing was a mile away from the bent-arm, swaying, slashing style of the old Scottish pros which had become the accepted style of the 1890s. He was a quiet, good-mannered, rather taciturn man with huge hands, a different type from his friend Ted Ray, who was characterized by his reply to a request for guidance to longer driving: 'Hit it a bloody sight harder, mate.' Vardon, who was much admired by Bobby Jones, had this verbal exchange when they first played together in 1920. Jones hit a poor, thin shot which scuttled over the green and in his youthful exuberance called out: 'Did you ever see a worse shot than that, Harry?' 'No,' said Vardon, and played the rest of the round in silence. But for a sudden gale which ruined his last 9 holes, he would have won the US Open at the age of fifty, and in the next year, at the age of fifty-one, he won both of his

Right: *A print of Ted Ray, the 'Jersey Giant'*

QUITE A NICE CHANGE: A NEW GOLF CHAMPION.
The Up Swing
The Champion
The Down Swing
And a walk of 350 Yards
Frank Reynolds

Massy -
- a back
view.
"Who Cares?"
Massy bears his
defeat with equanimity.
Braid
slightly
desperate.
Harry Vardon
watching a
short approach.
Ray
taking
things
easy.
H. H. Hilton
makes a desperate
effort.

matches against the US Professionals at Gleneagles. If he had not had two attacks of tuberculosis in the period 1905–10 and been stopped by the outbreak of World War I, who knows how many championships he would have won. And with all this he only did a single hole in one.

But look at the record. Only three Britons have won both the British and the US Open Championships: Vardon, Ray and Jacklin – and two of them Jerseymen.

Today the Channel Islands flag is carried by Tommy Horton, of Jersey parentage but born an evacuee in England during World War II. Horton, who is now attached to the Royal Jersey Club, has had a distinguished professional life, including membership of the Ryder Cup and World Cup teams. I remember him best in the golden weather at the Turnberry Championship in 1977, when his was the only British name to appear amid eleven Americans on the leader board. He won local championships in Africa and many tournaments at home and abroad and was elected Chairman of the Professional Golfers' Association. A worthy successor.

Left: *Harry Vardon, Open champion for the fifth time at Sandwich in 1911*

CHAPTER 9

Commonwealth and Empire

The British Empire, which reached its zenith in the twenty years before World War I, spreading its dominions, colonies and protectorates across the globe in a display of power and influence inconceivable today, began its climb to world domination three hundred years before, when England, which had earlier taken over Wales, finally turned its back on France and was united with Scotland under one Sovereign in 1603.

The first union flag was designed in 1606, and after 150 years which produced a fair crop of disagreements the Union with Scotland settled down under a single parliament. Similarly Ireland, which had suffered various degrees of independence, suppression, occupation and civil war for centuries, was finally brought into the United Kingdom by the Union of 1801, and the Irish red diagonal was added to the Union flag.*

From the middle of the eighteenth century until the Treaty of Versailles after World War I the growth of empires, not only ours but half a dozen others – not least the Russian – proceeded apace. Apart from the shocking loss of the American colonies, British territories overseas multiplied and great new nations emerged from them: Canada, Australia, New Zealand and even South Africa, once hostile, formed, it seemed, strongholds of British standards and the British way of life, and, glowing as 'the Brightest Jewel in the Crown', there was India.

Yet all the magnificence and power, 'the White Man's burden', 'dominion over palm and pine', the 'lesser breeds without the law', all was dead and gone in a generation and 'all our pomp of yesterday was one with Nineveh and Tyre'.

Two world wars, each fought from the first day to the last, had wrecked this glittering display and the Wind of Change blew through the ruins.

Ireland was the first to go, split in 1921 into a self-governing dominion of twenty-six counties in the south, with six counties in the north remaining in the United Kingdom. It was not long before the Free State cut adrift altogether as an independent republic and then remained neutral in the war with Hitler.

Then India was liberated and partitioned with horrifying bloodshed, and once India was gone there was nothing to set against the natural human belief that it was preferable to be badly governed by men of your own race than well governed from London.

What has survived is that most extraordinary association, consisting at present of forty-nine nations, known as the Commonwealth, a mixture of almost every variety of government, from orthodox parliamentary democracy under the Queen to military dictatorship and Marxist one-party rule. Members of the Commonwealth have at times made war on each other, and the only common factor seems to be that each was once part of the British Empire. Some

* Oddly enough the smallest parts of the British Isles, the Isle of Man and the Channel Islands, were not incorporated in the United Kingdom and have remained semi-autonomous though close associates under the monarchy.

An old print of golf in Calcutta shows that the hazards include snakes and vultures

eighteen in number acknowledge the Queen as head of state, the others do not, but allow that the Queen is the titular head of this strange body which they are glad to belong to, however much they may scold and abuse the Old Country.

Seemingly this is all a long way from the game of golf and farther still from Royal Golf, but the association is there and it goes back to the palmy days of pomp and circumstance and Empire. Then British settlers, soldiers and administrators went to the four corners of the earth and they took with them their laws and customs, their trade and progress and their games and pastimes. Golf was early one of these, and in every corner of the Empire it flourished.

With the game came its style and titles, and the desire for royal patronage and recognition was as strong and as sought after in New South Wales as in East Anglia. While the royal titles which were granted to clubs in the Empire make an intelligible group on the map of fifty years ago, today when the Empire has disappeared some of the titles which survive have ended up in surprising surroundings. Many are in the Commonwealth, which is not unexpected, and are honourably retained even in the republican group of countries. More surprising is the survival of the British royal titles proudly borne by clubs in nations no longer in any way related to us.

INDIA

Without doubt India holds a most honourable place in the development of the game outside the British Isles. Indeed, excepting Blackheath and the more shadowy presence of Old Manchester, the golf clubs of Calcutta and Bombay rank next in date only to the golf clubs of Scotland.

Royal Calcutta

It is the saddest thing that no written records exist of this most famous club earlier than 1876. I had hoped for a rich store of history from the oldest golf club outside the British Isles dating back to the days before the British Raj, to the old East India Company, almost to Warren Hastings, who died only one year before the club was born. Not so; and we must be content with the Club's own words in its 150th anniversary book: 'It has been established that the Royal Calcutta Golf Club was founded in the year 1829 and that it had its beginnings at Dum Dum, then a small suburb to the north-east of Calcutta.'

Starting then at Dum Dum, where the Calcutta International Airport now is, with 15 holes, the Club 'at some later date removed itself to the Maidan, that vast expanse of open grassland which still exists, in spite of several inroads, in the middle of the city'. Golf lasted many years on the Maidan, but the Club also started to use a new course at Dum Dum in 1892.

The Maidan years were times of important growth for the Calcutta Club; a trophy was presented to them in 1874 by Royal Blackheath, who had been helpful friends from the beginning, and a cup given in return. Trophies were also given and received with the Royal and Ancient in St Andrews in the 1880s. An Amateur Championship week was inaugurated at Dum Dum and the Maidan by the Club at Christmas in 1892.

In spite of this, and in spite of being a substantial full-length 9-hole course, Dum Dum didn't long survive and the Calcutta Club decided to look for new premises altogether. After a spell as guests at the Barrackpor Club and protracted negotiations, land was bought at Tollygunge on the south side of Calcutta, close to the golf club already there, in 1908 and 1909. In November 1910 the first 9 holes of the new course were opened with a match, 'and a splendid breakfast was provided'.

The course on the Maidan was kept going, although it was reduced in size by the construction of the Victoria Memorial in 1903, and it survived until the outbreak of World War II.

In 1911 King George V and Queen Mary were in India for a royal Durbar at Delhi, and during the visit the Club applied through the Viceroy, Lord Hardinge, for the privilege of using the title 'Royal'. At a meeting on 18 December 1911:

> a letter was read out from Major Wigram and another from the Private Secretary to the Viceroy advising that the club's application for the use of the title 'Royal' should be forwarded to the local Government for submission to the Secretary of State. The letter should be accompanied by a short history of the club and certain other information regarding its present strength and so on. But it was not until 5th November 1912 when R. Duncan, the Captain of the club, read out a letter to his Committee from the Hon'ble C. J. Stevenson-Moore C.V.O. I.C.S. Chief Secretary to the Government of Bengal, that he could inform the club that His Imperial Majesty, the King Emperor had been graciously pleased to grant the title of 'Royal' to the Calcutta Golf Club in commemoration of their Majesties' visit to Calcutta in the early part of the year. A letter conveying the Committee's deep appreciation of the privilege was thereupon addressed to Stevenson-Moore with the request that a copy be forwarded to His Majesty.
>
> That the club continues to incorporate the title 'Royal' with a certain pride to this day is difficult to reconcile with the fact that the announcement appeared as item 8 in the minutes and was almost lost in a welter of comparatively inconsequential deliberations; the writer had to watch diligently before he came across it.*

* The Club's History 1829–1979, p. 31.

The full 18 holes of the Old Course were completed and opened for play in December 1912. The course had been hacked out of the jungle and woodland, and its construction with a few tools was a considerable and lengthy affair.

A splendid club house was added in 1914 to match the full opening of the 18 holes in 1913 with extensions after World War II.

World War I had hardly affected the Club, apart from the loss of thirty-six members killed in action in various theatres. Royal Calcutta prospered after the War, and a new course was built by 1925, but, like the new course at Addington at home, it did not outlive the old, disappearing in 1972.

The Club continued its prosperous way until the inevitable disruption of World War II and all the subsequent unrest and changes in India. One notable change was that only in 1946 were the first Indian members admitted to Royal Calcutta, a fact which is 'hardly believable forty years on'.

Pressure on living space in Calcutta eventually forced the club to dispense with the New Course, and what is left now is an improved full-length, first-class course, flat inevitably in this estuarine area but well bunkered with well-made-up greens and large water hazards known as 'tanks' as a special feature.

Special too are some huge and magnificent trees. My recollections of a round there some years ago are of lush grass, of flatness but not simplicity, and of the tanks and trees as something rare and splendid.

It is good to report that after the independence of India in 1947 and its subsequent transformation from a dominion to a republic in 1950 the respect for the royal title has remained and the Club has marked royal occasions suitably, expressing sympathy at the death of King George VI in 1952 and sending congratulatory telegrams to the Queen on her birthday.

Royal Bombay

Founded in 1842, this club was second only to Royal Calcutta as the oldest club outside Great Britain. Unfortunately Royal Bombay is no longer active, having folded up in 1947 after years of uncertain existence. The name has survived, though, without a golf-course, c/o the Gymkhana Club of Bombay.

There seems to have been a break in the Club's existence between 1847 and 1855, and it lapsed again from 1861 to 1869, at which point we read that on 16 November 1869 'Messrs Robert Stevenson and Edward Morris in concert with other energetic admirers of the "noble game" reconstituted the club under the name of the Royal Bombay Golf Club'.* By whose good graces the royal title was bestowed is not recorded.

In the active days of the Club the game was played with increasing difficulty on the public open spaces of the city, sharing the ground with polo, hockey, football and cricket. Here canvas bunkers were used as hazards, set up early each morning and removed at noon, as play was restricted to mornings only.

Royal Blackheath was quick to welcome the Bombay Club, in a minute recorded in August 1842, ordering a bumper to be filled to drink success to their new colleague and sending a copy of the rules.

The Bombay Club presented a silver medal to the Royal and Ancient Golf Club at St Andrews in 1845, and in response it was resolved that the Captain of the Bombay Club should be an honorary member of the R & A. This medal is regularly played for by R & A members at the spring meeting, and it is sad that the donor club has not survived.

Royal Western India, Nasik

This, alas, is another royal club which has not survived. It was started at a summer resort 2000 feet up on the Deccan Plateau about 120 miles from Bombay on the road to Delhi. For many years it housed the Western India

* *The Golfing Annual*, Vol. XXII (1908–9).

Championship. The Club was founded under the patronage of the Duke of Connaught, a famous supporter of the game in the 1890s.

CANADA

Golf as we know it today came to North America with the many Scots who settled in Canada in the nineteenth century and so began well ahead of the start of the game in the United States several years later. It is true that, as Grimsley's history of American golf states, 'Research of the period immediately following the Revolutionary War has uncovered newspaper references to "golf clubs" and "golf greens" but no record of golf competitions. The clubs apparently were purely social.' These special references were found in newspapers in Charleston, South Carolina, and Savannah, Georgia, between 1795 and 1830, but referring only to balls, parties and social events. David Stirk in his new work *Golf: the History of an Obsession*, however, produces some concrete evidence that golf was in fact played here, though it died out.

We need not pay too much attention either to the sporadic attempts to get the game of golf organized in Quebec and Montreal, though I was particularly pleased to learn from a newspaper report that in the exceptionally mild winter of 1824 'a few true sons of Scotia . . . have fixed upon December 25 and January 1 for going to the Priests' Farm to play golf', because for three happy years we lived in a small colony of houses on the Priests' Farm in Montreal, and what's more next-door to the home of a mother and daughter each of whom had been Lady Champion of Canada, Dora and Judy Darling – a combination matched only I think by the British Ladies' Championships of Mme Lacoste of France and her daughter Catherine.

We can ignore too 'the claims to pioneer honours of a young Glasgow sailor named William Dibman who, finding himself in the Port of Quebec in 1854, "carried his clubs to the Heights of Abraham and there entertained himself in solitary contentment" ', to quote Robert Browning's *History of Golf*, and turn our attention to America's first *club*, the very first of – how many today? – 1000 in Canada and 13,000 in the United States, I believe.

Royal Montreal

Here is where golf really began in America, when, on 4 November 1873, a meeting of eight men in an office near the Montreal docks formed the Montreal Golf Club. The 'Father of Golf in Canada' on this occasion and for many years was Alexander Dennistoun, a Scot of proud lineage and royal connections and a huge man into the bargain.

The formation of the Club was the consequence of the city's purchase of the great cliff of Mount Royal, which so superbly dominates Montreal, for use as a public park; and, on a flat part of this land, at the eastern end (which is now bestrode by Park Avenue) known as Fletcher's Field, the golf club began its life with play on Saturday 7 November. Originally 6 holes were laid out, later 9, and their positions in the park altered from time to time. It was not long before play on this public land became inconvenient and incapable of meeting the growing needs of both golf club and city.

In 1896 the Club, by this time Royal Montreal, bought land far out in the country at Dixie, 10 miles to the west of the city, and laid out two fine 18-hole courses astride the two railway lines of the Canadian Pacific and what was later the Canadian National Railways – safe, it would seem, from urban encroachment. Not so: the growth of Dorval and later the huge international airport and the development of metropolitan Montreal put Dixie under developers' pressure, and once more Royal Montreal moved further out – abandoning its huge palatial club house to a religious order – to the rural calm of the small island known as Ile Bizard 10 miles

Royal Montreal, where golf really began on the American continent

further out to the north-west. Here the Club has come to rest on a splendid site of 800 acres of rolling farm land and maple bush near the Lake of Two Mountains, with a modern club house of lavish proportions and 45 holes of excellent and exacting golf laid out by the late Dick Wilson. Luckily the increased value of the Dixie site matched the cost of developing Ile Bizard, and the transformation was done so quickly that in under two years play was possible at the new site, which became fully operational in the summer of 1959.

There is little doubt that the Club is immensely better off in its new home, away from the roar of the road and rail traffic and the scream of jet engines. The golf is much better, with some splendid golf-holes on both Blue and Red courses and a more modern and less pretentious club house which still can put up those Canadian characters, the summer bachelors known as the Boarders – though these I suspect are a diminishing group.

When I first saw the Ile Bizard club just after it was opened, the courses looked rather bare and meadowy, although the quality of many of the holes, especially the now-famous water holes, was unmistakeable and the demands of the built-up greens severe. However, now that the trees which have been planted have begun to grow, it will, I am sure, have become a place of rare quality, with its nearby lake and surrounding hills.

And this is as it should be, the premier club of Canada and of all America should indeed be nobly housed, and Royal Montreal is just that.

Many important events have been played here and its club matches with Royal Quebec, Toronto, Royal Ottawa and the

Country Club at Brookline, Massachusetts are venerable and indeed ancient institutions. Its support of the Royal Canadian Golf Association has also been decisive. Well has Royal Montreal deserved its title, which it has now held for over a hundred years since Queen Victoria granted it in 1884.

A return after 25 years showed that much that was remembered still remained and indeed that the admirable belief in letting well alone had obviously prevailed here. In consequence Dick Wilson's two fine courses, seen from a cart kindly propelled by John Franklin, were familiar ground, especially the water holes, the 4th on the Red and the 16th and 17th on the Blue. A big improvement over the years has been the growth of the trees, and exceptionally fine specimens are now everywhere, particularly my favourites, the maples, which not only delight us in the autumn but wear such a handsome shape at all seasons.

Next day, as we drove out of Montreal to Mirabel Airport along Park Avenue, we passed by Fletcher's Field, where the first golf club in America started play in 1873. On a brilliant spring evening it looked green and well kept, indeed well fitted to provide some simple form of the game even today. Its location under the shoulder of the great mountain of Mount Royal, topped by its huge cross, is a handsome one. This brief view of the historic turf reminded us of our vision of the city as we flew from Britain to live here nearly thirty years ago, when on a freezing cold morning we sighted the huge lit cross under our wings and the million lights of the city.

Royal Quebec

Second only to Montreal, and close on its heels, the Quebec Golf Club with the usual Scots founder-members came to life in 1875, the second of all golf clubs in America. A moving spirit at the start was the sister of Old Tom Morris of St Andrews who was married and living there.

It will be no surprise to hear that play started on the open public lands of the Heights of Abraham next-door to the citadel of Quebec City where the battle for the colonial ownership of Canada was decided in 1759.

As usual golf on public park land was soon impossible, and in 1914 Royal Quebec moved out to an attractive site close to the Montmorency Falls. Nearby was Kent House, where the Duke of Kent, father of Queen Victoria, lodged from 1791 to 1794 with his faithful and loving mistress of twenty-seven years, Mme de St Laurent. Victoria spent the summer there the year before she became Queen.

Ejected by the owners, the Club had to move from Montmorency, and in 1925 settled in a wooded site on the Heights of Boischatel overlooking the Ile d'Orléans and the great St Lawrence river with the Laurentian Mountains behind.

Matches between Montreal and Quebec began as early as 1876, as the admirable book of the Royal Montreal Golf Club, *The Centennial of Golf in North America*, on which I have so much relied, tells us:

> For many years in the inter-club matches, the teams of golfers travelled between Quebec and Montreal on the overnight river steamers of happy memory. The unofficial records state that these journeys were characterised by long hours of blissful slumber, a prodigious consumption of lemonade and a complete absence of card games.

Royal Quebec received the title in 1933 from King George V.

Royal Ottawa

The Ottawa Golf Club was started in 1891 with a 9-hole course on rented land in Sandy Hill in the heart of the city, moving out in 1897 on account of housing developments. The ground the Club bought outside Ontario on the Quebec side of the river was found to have an excellent source of limestone for

The first Canadian Amateur Championship was played at Royal Ottawa in 1895

cement-making, so the Club sold out at a profit in 1904 and, continuing across the Ottawa river on the Quebec side, bought a tract of rolling woodland conveniently close to the city. It now covers 300 acres, with 27 holes of attractive golf.

The major Canadian championships have been played at Royal Ottawa, including the first Canadian Amateur in 1895 on the old Sandy Hill course for a cup presented by the Earl of Aberdeen, the Governor General of Canada. The winner was a Mr T. Harley of the Kingston Club.

In 1912 the uncle of King George V, the Duke of Connaught, Governor General of Canada, who was a keen golfer, sought permission for the royal title, which was granted in these terms:

Downing Street
May 29, 1912

Canada
No. 372
Sir
I have the honour to acknowledge the receipt to Your Royal Highness's despatch No. 271 of the 1st May, and to inform you that, in view of the special circumstances of the case his Majesty the King has been graciously pleased to approve of the Ottawa Golf Club styled 'The Royal Ottawa Golf Club'.

I have the honour to be, Sir
Your Royal Highness's most
obedient humble servant
(Sgd.) L. HARCOURT

The Governor General His Royal Highness
The Duke of Connaught & Strearearn, K.G., K.T., K.P., G.C.B., G.S.I., G.C.M.G., G.C.I.E., G.C.V.O., &c., &c.

The winner of the first Canadian Open Championship played at Royal Montreal in 1904 was J. H. Oake of the Ottawa Club.

A personal visit in the best of spring weather in late May showed us that here was a parkland course of quality, brilliantly green with splendid trees, mature, well shaped and elegant, and a profusion of flowering shrubs. The course has a good variety of terrain, with plateaux, hollows, streams and rolling slopes to give an interesting layout, far from flat and dull.

I had the good fortune to be taken round in a cart by Tom Mann, the pro here, who in 1989 was destined to be the President of the Canada PGA, no less. He gave me a new informal 'royal' title to work with, in the USA, as the CPGA has founded a club near Cape Canaveral in Florida to give work for the Canadian professionals in the winter when their home clubs are snowed in. They decided to call it the Royal Oak, a nice tribute to Charles II's escape from his foes in the Civil War in 1650, when he hid in a tree after the disastrous battle of Worcester. Although not a royal club by the rules of this work, it is good to know that the name has been used, and in the USA at that.

State Governor Sir George Tom Molesworth Bridges, who received the King's approval in 1923 to give Royal Adelaide its royal prefix

Royal Colwood

The last of the Canadian Royals is the Colwood Club in British Columbia near Victoria, the Provincial Capital, on Vancouver Island, one of the loveliest places on earth.

The Founding Fathers of the club in 1913 were Robert Dunsmuir and Joseph Sayward, and the Club has occupied its original site now for seventy-five years. The royal connection comes from visits by the Prince of Wales in the late 1920s and early 1930s, which led to the grant of the royal title by King George V in 1931. Pat Fletcher, the last Canadian to win the Canadian Open (in 1954), was a member here until he died in 1986.

This completes the list of genuine royal golf clubs in Canada, but we should add to the list the Royal Canadian Golf Association, which was founded in 1895. In 1896 its petition to use the prefix 'Royal' was granted by Queen Victoria. This style was maintained until 1948, when it applied for letters patent and its name now appears as the Canadian (Royal) Golf Association.

The associated body, the Canadian Golf Foundation, has confirmed that certain clubs or associations in Canada which carry the word 'Royal' as part of their title (examples of which include names in Calgary, Muskoka, Downs and Royal Oak) are not eligible by our definition for inclusion as royal clubs. I remember playing one such on my first visit to Canada fifty-five years ago: the Royal

York Golf Club in Toronto, which derived – and later changed – its name from the Royal York Hotel.

AUSTRALIA

Australia is blessed with a climate suitable for outdoor games the whole year round – compared with which Canada, except for parts of British Columbia, has to make do with only six or seven months of the year suitable for golf. In spite of this the number of golf clubs per million of the population of Canada is surprisingly high, but nothing like as high as in Australia, where the figure probably leads the world. Climate and native inclinations have made Australia the most sport-loving and sport-winning country for its size in history: look at the record, in cricket, lawn tennis, rugby football and half-a-dozen other sports, with golf well in the honours list.

The golf, of course, is where the people are, and as most Australians live in cities on the coastal rim of the continent it is not surprising to find the eight royal clubs of Australia dispersed thus:

		Date founded
1	Royal Adelaide	1870/1892
2	Royal Queensland	1890
3	Royal Melbourne	1891
4	Royal Sydney	1893
5	Royal Perth	1895
6	Royal Hobart	1900
7	Royal Fremantle	1905
8	Royal Canberra	1926

On most of these clubs the blessing of excellent sandy soil, almost linksland, is bestowed, such as you find in the famous sand belt to the south-east of Melbourne and in the country south of Sydney, towards Botany Bay.

Royal Adelaide

Golf was obviously played in Australia in a haphazard, disorderly way (as in Canada) in the early, nineteeth-century days of the colonies by Scotsmen resident or visiting, and reports of golf being played in Melbourne, Sydney and Geelong can be found.

Mr Cudmore of the Royal Adelaide Club has been kind enough to send me an account of its history which is so clear and satisfactory that I am reproducing it in full:

> The first Adelaide Golf Club started with a nine-hole layout on the Victoria Park Racecourse, immediately east of the city, in 1870. It appears to have lapsed at the end of the term as Governor of the colony in 1873 of Sir James Fergusson, who had provided the clubs and balls used.
>
> The present club started with an inaugural meeting at the Pier Hotel, Largs Bay, on August 11th, 1892, and the course in the north-east parklands, near the city, was opened on October 8th, 1892.
>
> This course was situated opposite the house then occupied by the distinguished British scientist William Henry Bragg (knighted in 1920), who had arrived in the colony in 1886 to become the first professor of experimental physics and the second professor of mathematics at the University of Adelaide.
>
> He became a keen player on the parklands course on which the narrow fairways were no more than the natural pasture cropped by grazing cows and the greens were cut by scythe.
>
> In 1896 that course was abandoned and the club moved to the seaside suburb of Glenelg, where it acquired a lease.
>
> In 1904 it was resolved to move once again, this time to Seaton, also close to the coast on the western side of the city, where there became available an ideal site for a links-type course which has become the club's permanent home.
>
> Bragg, who had become the club's secretary–treasurer in 1894, and who had at one stage reduced his handicap from 13 to 1, played a prominent part in designing the new course, which was officially opened by the State Governor, Sir George Ruthven

LeHunte, on June 30th 1906. Later the course was redesigned by that distinguished architect Dr Alister Mackenzie of Augusta fame.

The course, which has a railway line passing through it (12 holes on one side and 6 on the other) and which for many years had a platform near the clubhouse at which members and visitors from the city could alight, has hosted 13 national amateur championships and 8 Australian Open championships (the first in 1910).

A move to obtain the royal title at about the time of the move from Glenelg to Seaton failed.

The King's approval of the right to use the title prefix Royal was received in 1923 in a letter signed by Mr. Legh Winser, the private secretary to the State Governor Lt-Gen. Sir George Tom Molesworth Bridges (who reappears in this book later).

Winser was himself a distinguished golfer who had won the national amateur, State and club championships in 1921. He later went round in 80 on his 80th birthday.

All the main Australian tournaments have been played here, and all the great Australian golfers have performed at Seaton. Like all countries which offer good golf, Australia has produced players of international renown capable of taking on the best in the world – Von Nida, Pickworth, Ferrier, Kel Nagle, Bruce Devlin, Greg Norman, David Graham, who won the US Open, and best of the lot Peter Thomson, winner of the British Open no fewer than five times.

Royal Queensland

This club, the pioneer in the Brisbane area, originated in 1890 on a site south of the river at Yeerongpilly long since abandoned. Its proper history starts in 1920–1, when the area now occupied by Royal Brisbane at Hamilton north of the river and east of the city was developed for golf. The story is of 'routs and discomfitures, rushes and rallies' in the words of the Harrow song, with frequent changes made to the course and a long campaign fought to make a fine piece of golfing territory out of a very harsh and umpromising piece of land.

As the club did not own the freehold of the site it occupied, developments of the city and threats of developments necessitated changes of layout apart from those decreed by the membership. One change in 1926–7 was made on the advice of the celebrated Dr Alister Mackenzie, and two of his short holes, the 8th and 14th, have survived. The construction of a bridge over the Brisbane river spanning the course is the latest development to affect the Club and gives rise to a special local rule at the 12th hole, at which the tee-shot is played through an arch of the bridge with relief if the player hits it.

The growth of the club on its riverside site and the fulfilment of its plans to plant decorative trees and shrubs have been a success story, making this a championship course of rare distinction and beauty. The royal title was conferred early in the Club's history, late in 1921 after the first 18 holes at Hamilton were opened.

Royal Melbourne

Golf came and went in Melbourne in the 1840s, the Club such as it was ending with a dinner at the Royal Oak Hotel in 1850. After that the discovery of gold in New South Wales and Victoria caused a huge boom and influx of people, followed by slump, which put aside most frivolous activities, so that organized golf was not revived in Melbourne until 1891.

The Melbourne Golf Club which was formed that year subsequently divided into two, one of which today is the Royal Melbourne Golf Club and the other the Metropolitan Golf Club.

The split was caused by disagreement among the members about moving from the original site occupied by the club at Caulfield. One group, led by J. M. Bruce (of whom more in a moment), moved out to

Sandringham, not far from the sea, taking with them the royal title which had been granted in 1895. The new course was opened in 1901. The other club remained on-site as the Caulfield Golf Club, but later in 1908 moved out to the sand-belt area and became known as the Metropolitan Club, which flourishes today.

The original rules adopted were those of the Royal Eastbourne Club. At the instance of the Club the Earl of Hopetoun, Governor of Victoria, requested that the royal title should be granted. In reply from the Colonial Office in Downing Street, Lord Ripon on 1 June 1895 informed the Governor that Queen Victoria had approved.

The Royal Melbourne Club, after a rough time in the Great Depression stoutly faced, has prospered at Sandringham and today stands second to none in Australian, indeed in world, golf. It has grown to two courses of the highest class, and these are combined to make 18 holes of exceptional quality for big events. The Ti trees and mimosa scrub which line the rough at some holes are a rare sight for European eyes.

All the big tournaments have been played here, notably the World Cup (once known as the Canada Cup), which was played here in 1959 and again in 1972 and 1988. Not only did Australia win the Cup for the second time in 1959 with the team of Thomson and Nagle, but Peter Thomson tied with Stan Leonard of Canada for the best individual score. The equally prestigious tournament for amateurs, the Eisenhower Trophy, was held here in 1968, when the United States just beat Great Britain and Ireland and Michael Bonallack tied for the individual low score.

The originator of the plan to found the Melbourne Golf Club was J. M. Bruce, the father of S. M. Bruce, who became in turn the Prime Minister of Australia, Australian High Commissioner in London, Viscount Bruce of Melbourne and Captain of the Royal & Ancient Golf Club of St Andrews. Lord Bruce had promised to open ICI's new parkland course at Wilton Castle when he was Captain of the Royal & Ancient; but, as the opening had to be delayed, Lord Bruce, no longer Captain at St Andrews, declined the honour. To my horror the honour descended upon me, with the prospect – mercifully without the St Andrews cannon – of driving the first ball in front of a substantial and critical audience.

As Edward Prince of Wales has admitted, he fortified himself for his ordeal of playing himself in at St Andrews by, for the first and only time in his life, taking a dram. I must admit a similar recourse to the bottle – two drams in my case – and succeeded in hitting just about the best shot of my life. The moral is, I think, if there is one, that this is one of those rare occasions when two are better than one; if HRH had had a couple he might have hit as good a shot as his brother did eight years later.

That mine of information the *Shell International Encyclopedia of Golf* gives a good account of Royal Melbourne's opening play in 1901:

> The Lieutenant Governor Sir John Madden opened the new course on 27th July 1901. Sir John excelled himself in his speech but when it came to driving the first ball, he performed less gracefully. As Royal Melbourne's Official History relates, 'he was not endowed with any great facility for the game nor had he made any attempt to remedy by art his natural infirmities as a golfer.' He is recorded as announcing that he had never played the game before. In top hat and tail coat he hit an air shot which to make matters worse, the camera caught for posterity.

It was at Royal Melbourne that the apparently high proportion of left-handed golfers in Australia was brought home to me when I played in a match behind a fourball, all of them left-handed – a sight I thought as rare as a left-handed violinist.

Royal Sydney

Good linksland was abundant to the south of the city of Sydney in the years when golf was suddenly taking hold as a pastime. First in the field was what was and still is simply known as the Australian Golf Club, which can trace its origins back to 1882. As the pioneer, like the Country Club at Brookline, Massachusetts, or, in another sphere, the British postage stamp, it thus has no need to specify its location in its title. Next in the field was the Sydney Golf Club, now the Royal Sydney, formed in 1893. As, alas, I don't know this club, though I have had many enjoyable games at the Australian and other links courses round Sydney, it seems to me that I cannot improve on the narrative of the Secretary, obviously a kinsman, who sent me this account:

> The Club was formed with 20 members in August 1893 and its first location was at Concord in the inland Western Suburbs of Sydney.
>
> However members were extremely keen to have a links course and, by the end of 1893, they were playing at Concord and also at Rose Bay. Eventually, Concord was abandoned in 1899.
>
> In 1897, His Excellency Viscount Hampden, Governor of the state of New South Wales, opened the first Clubhouse at Rose Bay and presented the Club with a cup which became quite famous.
>
> Between 1897 and 1902 if you won the Hampden Cup you automatically won the Amateur Championship of New South Wales. It is now played for by members of The Australian and The Royal Sydney Clubs and winning it is much prized.
>
> On opening the Clubhouse in 1897 Viscount Hampden announced that he had received a despatch from Mr. Joseph Chamberlain, Secretary of State for the Colonies, addressed to Government House, Sydney, stating that Her Majesty had been graciously pleased to grant the Club the privilege of prefixing the title 'Royal' to its name.

In 1904, it was decided to build another Clubhouse. This one was destroyed by fire in 1920 and the present building was occupied in 1922.

Since its original formation with 20 members in 1893, the membership of the club has grown to 5,813, of which there are 3,256 male members and 2,557 female members. Its facilities include a championship course and a short nine-hole course, two practice areas, sufficient room for setting-down 16 lawn courts, 5 synthetic grassed courts which are also lit for night play, 2 croquet lawns, 2 lawn bowling greens and 2 squash courts. There is a full time Golf Professional with supporting staff and a full time Tennis Professional.

Inside the Clubhouse which is often described as 'a large cathedral like edifice' there are bars, lounges, card rooms, a snooker room and some 22 bedrooms. Although it was occupied in 1922 it was not until 1981 that a major extension was required to accommodate the growing membership. It is a much prized and exclusive venue for functions and nowadays it is no trouble to find a mother member arranging a wedding reception for her son or daughter in the same rooms in which her own reception was held.

Of the many benefactors and notable characters who have formed its membership, one E. P. Simpson stands out. He occupied the office of Captain from 1899 to 1930 and in 1920, when the office of President was created, he was elected to that office and then occupied both positions until 1930. He was a fine sportsman and was the fourth golfer to win the N.S.W. Amateur Championship. He was the last Captain to win office by play. His portrait painted by the famous Sir John Longstaff hangs in the Dining Room.

Various people contributed to the original lay-out of the courses. Even the famous Dr. McKenzie did some cross bunkering on certain holes. Recently the firm of Thomson, Wolveridge and associates updated the Championship Course when all greens were renewed along with a number of tees.

The major change in the course since its inception occurred in the fifties when a large number of trees were planted. Thirty years later the course is no longer a links but a parkland. Only certain links aspects remain. The open links land near the club has become built-up in a way reminiscent of what has also happened at St Annes at home.

The Club has been the venue for eight Open Championships of Australia, eleven Amateur Championships of Australia and nine Australian Women's Titles. In 1988, Australia's Bicentenary Year, the Open Championship of Australia will be held at the Club.

Royal Sydney has played a significant part in golf in Australia. Along with the Australian, Royal Melbourne, Royal Adelaide and Metropolitan Golf Clubs it formed the Australian Golf Union. Over the years it has provided men of high calibre with a great appreciation of golf and its traditions thus ensuring that the game in Australia has been properly developed through the club system.

by W. J. Allen (Secretary)

Royal Perth

Perth, the beautiful capital of Western Australia, once a remote town at the end of the line and now a rapidly expanding cosmopolitan city, is also favoured with a royal golf club.

The game was first played informally on Burswood Island in the Swan River, and here in 1895 the Perth Golf Club was founded. The golf was primitive, the course at times flooded and infested with weeds and the site inconvenient, so the club came ashore in 1900 to a farm at Belmont and finally to its present site in South Perth in 1908. Here the course was continually improved, until in 1934 it reached approximately its present layout.

The course is located in a sand belt near the Swan River, rather flat but an attractive site with, like most Australian clubs, good trees.

In the words of the club history book:

The year of 1937 was made memorable when a message was received from Colonel Manning (private secretary to Lieutenant-Governor Sir James Mitchell) that His Majesty King George VI had graciously granted the club the honour of calling itself the 'Royal Perth Golf Club.'

Royal Hobart

Far away at the other end of the Australian continent is the island of Tasmania, which can claim the earliest records of golf in Australia – as far back as 1830 or before.

The Hobart Golf Club started life in 1900 on a site now occupied by the campus of the University of Tasmania.

Like so many clubs, it began too close to town and moved out in 1916, and again to its present site 15 miles from the centre of Hobart at Seven Mile Beach near the airport, where in 1963 the new course was opened by the Governor of Tasmania, Sir Charles Gairdner. The course is on a level, undulating sandy soil with fine natural bush lining the fairways.

As the club records tell us:

Although the Governor of the day had always been the Patron of the club, a formal application to use the word 'Royal' was not made until 1907. A letter from the Secretary of State for the Colonies advised that permission could not be granted 'as the title Royal was to be confined to institutions devoted to National, Charitable and Scientific objects'. Another request was made in 1909, but it wasn't until very much later – 1925 – that the Hobart Golf Club became the 'Royal Hobart Golf Club'.

In 1924, Sir Herbert Nicholls, Chief Justice of Tasmania and club Patron, supported a request for the honour of a Royal Charter. Official notification from the Hon. Premier, also a letter from Lord Foster, the Governor General, were received in July 1925. It was resolved the Club colours be blue and gold with a badge consisting of a Crown over the letters R.H.G.C., and an 'Open Day' celebrating the club's Royal Distinction be held on November 14th, 1925.

The Australian Championships have been held at the new course, including the Open in 1971, when Jack Nicklaus won his third Australian Open.

Royal Fremantle

Although Perth, the capital of Western Australia, is close to the sea, it is not a port, and Fremantle a dozen miles down the coast has been developed to provide it. This is an attractive small town, with some well-preserved Victorian buildings and a royal golf club dating from 1905. The early development of the course in public park land was a struggle against limestone and rock covering, rough ground and water, and money shortages. The course has been altered from time to time to bring it up to modern standards. The club records tell us:

> In 1930 Club spirits were revived from a very different source. For some years Sir William Campion had been a constant visitor to the Club for which he had formed a very sincere attachment. It was reported to the Annual General Meeting of the year that:- 'The Club received information through His Excellency the Governor that His Majesty the King had graciously permitted the Club to use the prefix Royal, and as His Excellency was chiefly instrumental in obtaining for the Club, the distinction mentioned, the Committee took early steps to suitably express the appreciation of the Club to Sir William Campion.'

Royal Canberra

After World War I the development of a federal capital for Australia was pursued in earnest. Golf had begun in Canberra in 1913, but in 1924, 9 new holes of golf were laid out by the local authorities. In 1926 the Canberra Golf Club was formed, and the Prime Minister of Australia, Stanley Melbourne Bruce, whom we have met already, opened the 18-hole course in December 1927.

In 1933 the Prime Minister, Joseph Lyons, also a keen golfer, applied through the Governor General, Sir Isaac Isaacs, for permission for the Club to use the prefix 'Royal'. King George V approved and in the next year granted permission for the use of a crown in the Club's badge.

The original course was submerged by the big artificial lake which now graces the centre of Canberra, and a fine layout was constructed in Westbourne Woods, which was part of an arboretum first planted as far back as 1915. The new course was ready for play in 1962.

With two hundred varieties of tree, native and exotic, Royal Canberra is one of the most beautiful and attractive golf-courses in the world. No wonder Arnold Palmer said it was like Augusta National, home of the Masters.

SOUTH AFRICA

In these days it is often forgotten that the Union of South Africa – brought into being as a self-governing dominion by an act of statesmanship in 1910 which would heal, it was hoped, the wounds of the Boer War – was regarded as likely to become one of the great pillars of the Empire. A valued ally in two world wars, it seemed a partner of the true metal, but as the world moved on and the Empire dissolved South Africa became alienated from British sentiment and, for good reasons or for bad, with understanding of its problems or without, was separated from its Commonwealth associates and cast into isolation.

With the white tribe which settled in southern Africa, notably the British part, came many British and European customs, among them golf, and the game started in Cape Province, in Natal and around Johannesburg in the nineteenth century. The desire for royal recognition here was as strong as it was elsewhere in the Empire, and four clubs received the royal blessing; all, in spite of the upheavals of thought and political ties, retain their royal titles today and are proud of them.

Royal Cape, the first golf club in South Africa, against the backdrop of Table Mountain

The clubs are:

	Founded	Royal title
1 Royal Cape	1885	1910
2 Royal Johannesburg	1890	1931
3 Royal Durban	1892	1932
4 Royal Port Alfred	1907	1924

Royal Cape

This was the first golf club in South Africa and one which I remember with affection for its excellence, for it is a first-rate golf-course, for the splendid views of Table Mountain, an incomparable backdrop, and for the presence of large harmless mole snakes in the rough which were left there, no doubt in order to do what needs doing in my lawn at home. Also I seem to remember I played quite a good game.

The Royal Cape Golf Club owes its start to the arrival in South Africa on 5 November 1885 of General Sir Henry Torrens to command the British troops at the Cape of Good Hope. His energy and love for the game got things moving within nine days of his arrival. Later, in 1888, he moved on to be Governor in Malta and that year founded the Royal Malta Golf Club, which also survives to this day.

The game at the Cape started largely as a military affair on a crude 9-hole layout near the Wynberg Barracks on Waterloo Green. In 1891 the Club moved to almost equally coarse grounds with 9 holes on the Rondebosch Common, which it shared with the town rubbish dump, a Malay graveyard and the local rugby football club, the first in South Africa. Cecil Rhodes was an early member there, together with all the men of mark in Cape Town.

As so often happened, more room was needed and a private ground, so once again the Club moved, in 1906, to the excellent site it now enjoys at Wynberg Ottery. Here grass was used for the greens for the first time instead of gravel.

In 1910 the first Union Parliament was opened by the Duke of Connaught, representing his brother King Edward VII. The Royal Charter for the Club which commemorates this event was granted by the new King, George V, as stated in a letter from the Colonial Office in Downing Street, signed by L. Harcourt, to the first Governor General of the Union, Lord Gladstone, son of the former Prime Minister.

The Club prospered in the inter-war period and was enlarged and improved in 1928 to what was virtually a new course. It was modernized and improved again in 1967 and 1970 to its present state.

Royal Cape has produced a fine crop of good golfers, of both sexes, and has played a distinguished part in the development of South African golf. To mark its centenary in 1985, it elected South Africa's two greatest golfers, Bobby Locke, four times British Open Champion, and Gary Player, winner three times, and both of them with a huge array of other championships and titles, to honorary membership.

Royal Johannesburg

This club has the rare distinction – indeed unique, I think, at least among the royal clubs honoured by our royal family – of having had its President, Lionel Phillips, imprisoned under sentence of death and its first Captain, H. Becher, also in prison. They had been jailed for their complicity in the notorious and unsuccessful Jameson Raid in January 1896. This was intended to raise a rebellion against the independent Boer Republic of the Transvaal and redress by force the grievances of the unenfranchised immigrants the Uitlanders, by whom among other things the first golf club in Johannesburg had been created.

This was back in 1890 when the city was little more than a rough mining camp. Its rapid growth before and after the Boer War of 1899–1902 meant that the Johannesburg Golf Club had to move no fewer than five times and occupied six sites before settling in 1910 in the area where it is now. Even so, there have been numerous changes, including a complete re-orientation of two 18-hole courses in 1937. So the Club probably holds the record – at any rate among the royals – for having had more courses than any other, ten in all.

The present courses, two of full length and strength with attractive trees, notably the blue-flowering jacarandas seen in the colour picture, are enjoyable golf and the big modern club house as fine as any. All the major South African tournaments have been held here, and it can take its place among the elect. My correspondent, Mr H. Snow, gives the following account of the granting of the royal title here:

> H.R.H. The Prince of Wales holidayed in South Africa during the early part of 1930. In January or February he stayed briefly in Johannesburg both on his way north to Rhodesia and on his return south. It was probably on the latter that he played golf on our course at Orange Grove. The question of the grant of the Royal title must have been suggested then and the President of the Club at that time, Mr. Russell F. MacWilliam, must have written more or less immediately. Unfortunately we do not have the letter which was addressed to Admiral Halsey, comptroller to the Prince. 11 months later there was a reply saying that the Prince had graciously consented to be Patron of the Club and six months after that in July 1931, a date we do know, the President was able to announce that a letter had been received from His Excellency The Governor-General intimating that His Majesty The King's gracious assent to the prefix 'Royal' had been granted to the Club.

Royal Durban

This club in the capital of Natal province is not one which I have had the pleasure of visiting, but it has a venerable history dating back to 1892, when the Town Council gave permission for 9 holes to be laid out inside the oval of the race-course. And here to this day the Club resides.

The Club first gained distinction when the South African Championships were held here in 1911. Just before World War II a completely new layout was made to give a full-length modern course.

The royal title was conferred via the office of the Governor General of South Africa by King George V in 1932.

Royal Port Alfred

This is the fourth of the royal clubs in South Africa, with a seaside course with some linksland on the coast of Cape Province at Kowie West. In the latter part of 1907 a group of local businessmen put up £20 each to promote the building of 9 holes by convict labour, and play started at the year-end with shell-grit greens. By 1914 a new seaside site, with grass greens, was in use, with wild asparagus in the rough.

The club, which is essentially for holiday visitors, has been altered from time to time. The Governor General of South Africa, Prince Arthur of Connaught, petitioned the King in February 1924 for royal title, which was granted in February of that year.

CHAPTER 10

Wider still and wider

Leaving India and the great Dominions, noting that while Australia has eight royal clubs and Canada four, New Zealand has none, there are some former outposts of Empire which carry the royal title.

Royal Malta

For a hundred years now golf has survived in Malta, an unpromising arid place for the game. Climate apart, this small island has seen and endured many political and military upheavals in this time, as in the centuries before it. Once Malta was a key defensive base on the lifeline of the Empire, with a huge naval dockyard and a fleet based on it; then a pivot in the defence of Africa against Hitler and Mussolini, mercilessly bombed and bravely surviving with a George Cross for its honourable conduct. It has now retired into a quiet life as a holiday and marine resort under a republican regime in the Commonwealth.

The game was brought here by Sir Henry Torrens, who had started the game in South Africa before he became Governor in Malta in 1888. The terrain was to say the least unpromising: dry sand or rocks in summer with some rank weeds and coarse grass in the winter rains. None the less, a 9-hole golf-course of sorts was laid out amid the walls

Above and Right: *Alfred Earnest Albert, Duke of Edinburgh (1844–1900), second son of Queen Victoria, who was patron of Royal Malta*

and ditches of the lines of fortifications built long before by the Knights of Malta: a golf-course in fact in the ditch of the Hornwork of Florian. Walls 20 to 30 feet high in which your ball could lodge confined the narrow 20-yard fairways, and grassless greens completed the lack of similarity to anything known in Britain. It was reported as 'grand practice for the iron'.

All this pseudo-golf has now gone, and the course of the Royal Malta Club moved after World War I to the site of the race-course at Mersa on the outskirts of Valletta. With the years the development of grasses has reached the stage of providing a green course for nine months of the year, and there are plans to increase this. Prince Alfred, Duke of Edinburgh, the sailor son of Queen Victoria, became Patron of the Club at the start and with his patronage granted the royal title which, nationalistic politicians notwithstanding, survives to this day.

Royal Nairobi

The golf club at Nairobi, the first in Kenya, was founded in 1906 and has over the years developed from a primitive 9-hole layout with sand greens along the Ngong Road, about 3 miles from the city centre, to the modern, grassy, full-length course with watered fairways of today. As with many overseas clubs, the influence of soldiers was decisive at the start, in this case the King's African Rifles, whose grounds provided the land for the first 9 holes.

Wild beasts frequented the area in the early days and a marauding leopard was shot between the 14th and 15th holes in 1919.

In the beginning the Club was exclusively the white man's playground but these days all nationalities are welcome; Indian names seem to predominate.

The royal title was granted by King George V in 1935, the Jubilee year, and in 1936 he also granted his patronage to the Nairobi Club, in a letter from Lord Wigram, Keeper of the Privy Purse.

The course has many attractive trees, and when the air is exceptionally clear it is said that you can see the distant snows of Kilimanjaro, 19,565 feet high, more than 100 miles away.

Royal Harare

Here is a royal title which has survived the extremes of political change. From being once the Royal Salisbury Golf Club in Southern Rhodesia, the club became absorbed into the short-lived Rhodesian Federation, which then split up. Salisbury became the capital of the rebel unilaterally independent Southern Rhodesia under Mr Ian Smith, then the capital of newly independent Zimbabwe and was renamed Harare. Golf today keeps going in the Royal Harare Golf Club in a state under the political domination of a Marxist single-party government led by Mr Mugabe.

Golf began in Rhodesia in 1895 at Bulawayo, only two years after the Matabele War ended with the capture of Chief Lobengula's kraal. The club at Salisbury followed in 1898, when Salisbury was a shanty town which sprang up after the occupation of Mashonaland by the white pioneers in 1890.

The first Salisbury course was too close to the centre of town to survive, but today's attractive tree-clad course is only 2 miles out. When the move had to be made in 1901 an attractive area had to be excluded on account of the risk of malaria and blackwater fever

The club house at Royal Harare

from the Makabusi river site. Like so many, the Salisbury Club had to start with rough local grass, rocks, bad soil and shaggy greens, with no play possible in the wet season, but has developed over the years to an all-weather course of quality on which many of the world's greatest players have performed. Today the 18 holes cope with 40,000 rounds a year.

Edward Prince of Wales played at Salisbury in 1925, and in 1929 his father granted the royal title.

The Secretary, Mr Padbury, who has been good enough to send me the Club's 75th anniversary handbook, tells us:

> The course being fully fenced enables us to keep Duiker (a species of antelope) and many guinea fowl of which we are proud. Snakes abound in an outcrop of rocks near the 4th tee but rarely leave their habitat. Any stray shot played into the rocks is inevitably declared 'lost' as no caddie will venture into that area.

The Club held a special meeting of members to enable the name to be changed to 'Royal Harare Golf Club' on 21 February 1983 in the terms of the Government Names (Alteration) Bill, and the British High Commissioner was informed.

Royal Colombo

Golf has a venerable history in Ceylon – now Sri Lanka – as there is firm evidence of the game being played here by the Dutch settlers when they occupied the island between 1651 and 1706.

The modern game in Sri Lanka dates from the formation of the Colombo Golf Club in 1879, before the big golf explosion in England. The Club was started by British, mainly Scottish, merchants and soldiers and golf was played along with other games on the great open space known as Galle Face Green, flanked by the sea and overlooked by the famous Galle Face Hotel. The Club moved in 1897 to its own grounds – where it still resides – known as the Ridgeway Golf Links in honour of Sir West Ridgeway, the Governor of that date and a keen player who once had marched with Lord Roberts from Kabul to Kandahar.

Although an expatriate stronghold, the Club was soon to admit local members, notably from the de Saram family, whose sporting prowess has for generations been pre-eminent.

The royal title of the Colombo Club was reached only after long and, it seems, undercover negotiations. Starting in 1922, when the Prince of Wales visited Ceylon, the enterprise only came to a happy climax in 1928, when 'His Majesty was pleased to confer upon the Colombo Golf Club the privilege of using the prefix, "Royal".'

I didn't get a game of golf in Sri Lanka, but I did manage to have a look at one of its best courses at Nuwara Eliya, up in the mountains in the tea-growing country; on a wet evening it might have been Worplesdon or Pitlochry.

This club shares with Royal Colombo the principal competitions held in Sri Lanka, whose Amateur Championship preceded those of India and the United States.

Royal Singapore and Royal Island

Originally there were two royal clubs in Singapore: the Royal Singapore, founded in 1891, and the Royal Island, founded in 1927. These were amalgamated to form the Singapore Island Country Club in 1963. The older of the two, the Royal Singapore Golf Club, had its course at the race-track until 1924, when, after clearing a jungle site at Bukit of tigers and wild boars, 36 holes of good park golf emerged.

The Island Club, later the Royal Island Golf Club, when in 1936 the two royals merged under the Island title, built a new course, designed by Frank Pennink in 1970 on the Island site. The World Cup tournament was held in Singapore in 1969 and was won by Orville Moody and Lee Trevino for the United States, with Trevino gaining the individual prize.

A personal note here is that an old diary record shows a round played over thirty years ago on the New Course at Royal Singapore with borrowed clubs and shoes with such indirect heat through cloud cover as to cause sunburn through a shirt, all adding up to the depressing score of 88 strokes.

What is remembered even today is the presence in the rough and on the fairways of a low-growing sensitive plant whose leaves when touched instantly closed up.

Malaysia

This is a federation of a number of states, each with its own ruler, who elect one of their number to be the head of the Federal Government for five years. The state rulers, who have considerable powers, are selected in accordance with the customs of the various states. This constitutional structure has led to the proliferation of royal titles for golf clubs in Malaysia, matching perhaps the rapid growth of golf there among all races in the last twenty years. I am indebted to Tan Kok Kee, the Honorary Secretary of the Malaysian Golf Association, for helping me to disentangle the titles and to a distinguished leader of the British business community there, Annesley Keown, for some notes which follow.

At the top of the royal list for Malaysia stands the *Royal Selangor Golf Club* at Kuala Lumpur, whose title was granted in 1963 by our monarchy at home. The club was founded in 1893 and grew with time into a fine affair with two good courses. The Japanese during the occupation in 1942–5 all but destroyed the Club and courses, their interest in golf being a strictly post-war development. After the War the courses were restored, and the Club has returned to support first-class golf, with advice and alterations by Frank Pennink to the original Colt designs.

Tan Kok Kee's list of royal clubs in Malaysia is seen below, with Selangor perhaps a cut above the others whose titles were granted by the local Sultans.

		Date of Club	**Date of Royal Title**
	The Royal Selangor Golf Club	1893	1963
1	The Royal Johor Country Club Johor Baru	1968	1984
2	Kelab Golf DiRaja Sri Menanti Serembam	1983	1987
3	Kelab DiRaja Kampong Kuantan Bukit Rotan	1910	1981
4	Royal Perak Golf Club Ipoh	1900	1979
5	Royal Kedah Club Alor Setar	1909	1970
6	Royal Kelantan Club Kota Baru	1938	1975
7	Kelab Golf DiRaja Terengganu Istana Badariah		
8	Kelab Golf DiRaja Pahang Pahang	1959	1985

Mr Keown's notes are as follows:

> Although the game has flourished in both countries for almost a century the granting of the title 'Royal' to golf clubs in Malaysia and Singapore is of relatively recent origin. In Singapore a golf club was formed in June 1891 and in Kuala Lumpur a Selangor Club Members' Meeting was convened on 21 January 1893 to approve the inauguration of a local golf club. Prior to 1893 golf clubs already existed in Penang and Malacca but unfortunately records of their founding are not traceable. Most courses, coastal, inland and in the hill tracts were hacked-out of the all-pervading jungle. However, once established they soon became a delight to the eye and a challenge to even the best of golfers. In the early days a major

problem was the preparation and maintenance of fairways and good greens. Originally coarse 'cow' grass was the standard choice for both fairways and greens. In the 1920s 'cow' grass on greens was replaced by 'Bermuda' grass which possessed great durability in punishing tropical conditions. In the thirties a new grass was developed in Singapore, was given the name 'Serangoon' and widely used. The relative merits of 'Bermuda' versus 'Serangoon' are still hotly debated.

Interest in golf in South East Asia and in Japan has expanded enormously in the past 30 years or so. This has been particularly true in Malaysia and Singapore where the business communities, both local and international, along with government officials, members of the armed forces and public figures have mixed freely with Royal families and Prime Ministers. So keen has been the enthusiasm for the game that traditional Malay Rulers have gladly bestowed Royal titles upon leading golf clubs in their States. Ordinary club Members are proud of their 'Royal' status and jealously protect the good name and standing of their Club and of the long term interests of Golf. The Club houses of many of these 'Royal' clubs are magnificent buildings and as well equipped as any elsewhere. The Singapore Island G.C., as it exists today, is an amalgamation in 1963 of the original Royal Singapore and Royal Island Golf Clubs. The multinational membership of the new Club is almost without equal and the game goes from strength to strength much to the pleasure of the Prime Minister Mr Lee Kuan Yew who is both a keen and competent golfer.

Hong Kong

Golf started here in a small way in 1889, when a club was formed and golf was played in Happy Valley on Hong Kong Island. The club shared facilities with polo-players, footballers and the army and navy at drill. In

The club house of Royal Hong Kong at Fanling

1897 Queen Victoria granted the royal title to the Hong Kong Club, and in 1898 it opened an attractive little 9-hole course over the hills of the Island at Deep Water Bay, then only accessible by boat. The Deep Water Bay course has survived, and I have had the pleasure of playing on it, but golf disappeared at Happy Valley in World War II.

Royal Hong Kong's main attractions, however, are at Fanling, 23 miles north of Kowloon on the mainland, in the Leased Territories close to the Chinese border. The first course was laid out in 1911, then a second followed, and today, after the courses had been maltreated during the War and restored afterwards, there are three rounds of 18 holes there. In the early days the members rode out to Fanling in a private Pullman car of the Kowloon–Canton Railway which served breakfast, after which a fleet of rickshaws pulled them to the club.

The royal title was granted to the Hong Kong Club as the result of a letter addressed to HM Queen Victoria's Lord Chamberlain, which gave rise to the following reply to Sir William Robertson, the Governor of Hong Kong:

> Sir, reference to your dispatch of 20th July addressed to the Rt. Hon. The Lord Chamberlain the Earl of Lothian, I have the honour to inform you that your application being laid before the Queen, H.M. was graciously pleased, in view of your recommendations, to give permission to the Hong Kong Golf Club to be called the Royal Hong Kong Golf Club.

CHAPTER 11

Other Monarchies

The monarchies of two countries in Europe, Belgium and Spain, follow the practice of conferring royal titles on selected golf clubs and have honoured a fine group of royal clubs – ten in Belgium and no fewer than eleven in Spain.

Before we attend in some detail to these two leading supporters of the royal honours, it should be noted that the three Scandinavian monarchies have not conferred any royal titles on golf, nor has the monarchy of the Netherlands. Mention should be made of the *Grand Ducal Golf Club* of Luxembourg, which can legitimately join our party, and of two names in France and one in Italy which cannot.

First-hand knowledge of the Luxembourg Club has not been available, nor reported information either.

In France two royal names show up, the *Royal Evian Golf Club* on the Lake of Geneva and the *Royal Golf Club Dormaine Saint-Michel*, a new club near Pau under the shadow of the Pyrenees.

One of our most reliable agents, Molly Sisson, was able to confirm that the Evian club was one of the sports attractions offered by the Royal Hotel there, which was the limit of its regal status. The Royal Sant' Anna Club in Italy near Como is in this category, we think.

The new club near Pau seems to carry no royal connections, though it is not far from the old Pau Club, the oldest golf club on the Continent, founded in 1856 by British expatriates, and the oldest golf club outside the British Isles except those at Calcutta and Bombay.

BELGIUM

Royal golf in Belgium is well established. As far back as 1903 King Leopold II, a capable, far-seeing but unloved monarch, saw that trade with Britain, which he regarded as essential for his country, would be fostered by providing for visiting businessmen the 'opportunity of playing one of their favourite sports, golf'. He made available Crown land at Ostend and in the royal parkland on the outskirts of Brussels and set up clubs there; he also persuaded the Wagon-Lits Company to promote the forming of a golf club in the park of the Château Royal d'Ardenne at Dinant. All King Leopold's clubs are flourishing today, and six other royal clubs besides.

While neither King Leopold II nor his nephew King Albert, who succeeded him in 1909, played golf, it has been enjoyed by their successors, the best royal performers of the game in any country in the world. King Albert's son, King Leopold III, who came to the throne after the tragic climbing accident which killed his much loved and respected father in 1932, was a first-class golfer by any standards; with a handicap of one or scratch, he was genuinely good enough to hold his own in amateur championships in Belgium or France. He is the only reigning monarch to have played in a national championship – the Belgian Amateur at Zoute in 1939 – and his best performance was to reach the last eight in the French in 1949. At an open tournament at Ascona in 1946 he was the leading amateur player. He played a lot of golf before and after his abdication in 1951. Leopold III's second wife, the Princesse de

Above: *King Leopold III, pictured with his wife Princesse de Réthy, both first-class golfers*

Left: *King Leopold II of Belgium, promoter of golf in his country*

Réthy, was also a first-class golfer, good enough to win the Ladies' Championship of Italy in 1949. King Leopold's son, King Baudouin, who came to the throne in 1951, was also a very good player, with a handicap of about two at his best. He was good enough to play in the Belgian Junior Team and to represent Belgium in an international team match against Holland in 1960, in which he won his single.

There are ten royal clubs in Belgium. The rules to be complied with being that the club should have been in existence for fifty years (originally it was twenty-five years) and that it should apply to the Chamberlain of the royal household, who passes the application to the Sovereign, who then grants the title. The royal clubs are:

1	Royal Antwerp Golf Club	Founded	1888
2	Koninklijke Golf Club – Ostend	"	1903
3	Royal Golf Club de Belgique – Brussels	"	1906
4	Royal Zoute Golf Club – Knokke	"	1908
5	Royal Lakem Golf Club – Ghent	"	1909
6	Royal Waterloo Golf Club	"	1923
7	Royal Golf Club des Fagnes – Spa	"	1930
8	Royal Golf Club de Hainaut – Mons	"	1933
9	Royal Golf Club du Sart-Tilman – Liège	"	1939
10	Golf Club du Château Royal d'Ardenne – Dinant	"	1950

There is also a 9-hole course in the Royal Palace grounds at Laeken in Brussels, akin to the Windsor course at home.

There were formerly two royal clubs in the Belgian Congo, before it became Zaire, the *Royal Leopoldville Golf Club* and the *Royal Elizabethville Golf Club*. The royal titles lapsed in 1960 with independence, but Mr Duys, the most helpful and friendly Secretary of the Royal Federation, told me that golf still survives at these courses, now known as the Kinshasa Golf Club and the Lumumbashi Golf Club, and that at the former some sort of international event had been staged.

We should close this section, mentioning the Belgian governing body, the *Fédération Royale Belge de Golf*, founded in 1912, as it, like its Spanish counterpart, has its own royal title.

Royal Golf Club de Belgique

This, though not the oldest, is undoubtedly the premier club in Belgium, founded by King Leopold II himself. Work began in 1905 in a magnificent piece of Crown forest land at Ravenstein in a part of the Forêt de Soignes, close to the capital. The course was ready for play in 1906. The trees and shrubs alone would make the course famous, but the golf is first-class too.

The seventeenth-century club house is a historic building on the site of an earlier hunting lodge and farm of the Clèves family, built by the orders of Infanta Isabel of Spain. The Ravenstein estate changed hands several times and was owned by the Prince of Orange in 1826 before Belgian independence. Leopold II only acquired it in 1880 and then gave it to the nation, as we have seen, in 1903, on condition that it should not be altered or spoiled.

The first notable event held at Ravenstein was an international championship held on 2 June 1910. There was a tremendous field, including the great Triumvirate from Britain, plus Duncan, Ray, Tom Vardon and Sandy Herd. The winner was Arnaud Massy from France, who had won our Open at Hoylake in 1907 (the first foreigner to win it) and tied for first at Sandwich in 1911.

Two world wars passed over Belgium with attendant miseries, but golf at Ravenstein survived. In February 1941 the German Command in Brussels issued an order restoring the club to its 'German and Belgian members', adding that it was not to be used for exercising the troops or for riding.

Royal patronage here has extended to royal membership of the club. First-class professionals are attached, including Aubrey Boomer, the Jerseyman and Ryder Cup player, past ninety years old and living in Belgium at the time of writing, and Flory van Donck, Belgium's most famous player so far, well known all over the world.

Royal Antwerp Golf Club

This is the oldest club in Belgium, formed by a group of British residents in Antwerp in 1888.

The first course was located on ground owned by the military, together with a race-course. Military activities, especially on horseback, did not fit in with the golf, the holes themselves causing anxiety. After much searching, a new and more convenient place was found for the Club at Kepellenbos, about 12 miles north of the city, and in 1910 the Club was established there, with a course designed by Willie Park Jr, which was opened for play in 1912. Originally the Club adopted the rules of the Royal Wimbledon

King Baudouin of Belgium (back row wearing sunglasses) with a team of golfers in 1958

A print of golf at Royal Antwerp in 1895

Golf Club at home but accepted the St Andrews rules in 1894.

World War I and the occupation brought chaos and near-disaster, but, starting with eight of the pre-war membership, the Club recovered a prosperous condition. It held the Belgian Open in 1925 and in that same year received the royal title from King Albert. With the acquisition of more land in 1928, the Club called in Tom Simpson to redesign the course and add a supplementary 9 holes.

World War II created a new set of problems, but the Club managed to keep 14 holes in play during the occupation, while the others were ploughed up to grow corn. The liberation of the country north of Antwerp in 1944 produced a hideous V1 and V2 bombardment and created a souvenir in the form of a bunker at the 4th hole. The club house, empty and almost in ruins, was recaptured from the enemy by British and American troops, who later enjoyed some golf at Kepellenbos. With the usual problems overcome, the club staged the Belgian Open in 1954, and in 1956 the Joy Cup match of European professionals led by Van Donck against the team described in the club history as 'Les Insulaires', including Henry Cotton, Peter Alliss, Harry Weetman, Christy O'Connor and Eric Brown.

Royal Antwerp is located in flat, sandy, well-wooded country with heather in the rough. It has been described as like Worplesden, West Surrey, Camberley Heath or West Hill. Even on a chilly February day the course looked attractive and ready for a round while the warmth and hospitality of the club house encouraged the thought that it was still a bit early for golf. An old print of the club I had found in a copy of the old *Sporting & Dramatic Magazine* was well received.

Royal Zoute Golf Club

Our visit here was a rather less cheerful affair than at Royal Antwerp, but we were able to get a view of the course before the rain closed in.

Zoute is a coastal resort, along with Knokke close to Zeebrugge on the Belgian coast, a rich-looking resort town with fine hotels and villas. Although golf was played on the coast here as early as 1889, the present club was founded in 1908. Its course today lies inland from the shore and is by no means a links; more it gives the impression of estuarine golf with trees. There is a true links on the Belgian coast at Ostend, the course of the *Koninklije Golf Club, Oostende*, but time, weather and approaching illness prevented a visit.

British residents, as elsewhere, had founded the Zoute Club near the town and, following what has almost seemed a rule, moved out to better premises, in 1930. It was freed after World War II by British and Canadian troops, and the liberators subsequently helped to get the game going again. Since then tournaments and championships have come here and there are distinguished names among the players. A flourishing Artisans' Club is attached.

Royal Waterloo Golf Club and *Royal Golf Club de Hainaut* at Mons were due to be seen at first hand, not least because of their association with British history, but illness intervened and confined these notes to interpreting the written word.

Royal Waterloo

This club, now at Ohain, dates from 1923, starting with 9 holes of park golf. The course moved to the present site in 1960 and has now grown to 45 holes, with two full courses laid out by T. W. Hawtree. The courses are in wooded country behind the escarpment of the battlefield. Henry Cotton was appointed pro to the club in the 1930s. Today it is without doubt one of the biggest and best of the Belgian clubs. A formidable championship layout known as the 'Lion' runs to 7000 yards and more.

Another attraction, of course – *the* attraction indeed – at Waterloo is the sloping hillside where, on soaking wet ground on that Sunday, 18 June 1815, Napoleon finally came to the end of the line. Now numerous mementoes of the event mark the site, the great lion monument to the Prince of Orange and the Dutch contingent, the circular diorama of the battle and the museums including the waxworks in uniform. In spite of all this there can just be pictured, looking south from the slight summit behind which Wellington's squares had taken cover, those fields alive with noise and drama. Two of the many quotations attributed to the Duke at that time have stayed enjoyably in my memory. The first was when Lord Uxbridge, the leader of the British cavalry, had his leg blown off by a cannon ball: he said 'By God I've lost my leg', and Wellington replied 'Have you, by God.' The second was in reply to a question from Creevey before the battle as to how he thought it would go; pointing to a rather forlorn-looking British infantry soldier looking at the statues in the streets of Brussels, he said, 'It all depends upon that article there whether we do the business or not. Give me enough of it and I am sure.' And basically it did depend on it – and the timely arrival of Blücher's Prussians in the afternoon.

The Royal Club de Hainaut

This is outside the grimy industrial and mining area of Mons on the road to Ath. The golf club dates from 1933, built on good sandy loam amid trees, pines and birch in particular, and heather and broom in the rough. The course suffered badly in World War II, with the Luftwaffe using it to train bombers and the Americans building a prisoner-of-war camp there later. The Americans, with prisoner-of-war help, rescued the Club. Then after the War came recovery, and in 1967 the location of the Allied Headquarters SHAPE, nearby, added strength from American and British members of the team there.

The Club remains to be visited another day, as I had especially wanted to see Mons, where north of the town along the canal bank on that hot Sunday morning, 23 August 1914, the small professional British Expeditionary Force stood in the way of the overwhelming unpredicted and unheralded might of the German right wing trampling through Belgium in obedience to the Schlieffen Plan to destroy France. What remains of the place where our men, isolated and hopelessly outnumbered, had given a good account of themselves, and were later in orderly retreat, I had wished to see; but the wish remains unfulfilled.

One episode of the hideous days of the retreat from Mons and rearguard action has always caught my imagination. Major Tom Bridges, a squadron commander in the 4th Dragoon Guards, was the first British officer to encounter the German patrols, on 22 August. Subsequently, surviving injury in a cavalry charge on 24th, he was commanding the rearguard of the British Army after the battle at Le Cateau as it retired through Saint Quentin on 27 August. Finding the town full of exhausted stragglers, past movement and past caring, whose commanding officers had prepared an order to surrender, Bridges commandeered all the town's local transport and got away the wounded and the worst cases to the south. He was left after dark with five hundred demoralized and truculent men lying in the square, unwilling to be coaxed or cajoled into getting up to save themselves. Bridges and his trumpeter broke into a toy-shop and seized a drum and a tin whistle. These two then marched round the square playing 'The British Grenadiers', until the men at last began to respond. In the end the men *all* got up and in a semblance of order marched out of the town to safety and to fight another day. Leaving his horse, Bridges marched all night with them.

And here we come upon a pleasing consequence of relevance to this book. The King's approval for the title 'Royal' to be used by the Royal Adelaide Golf Club in far-off Australia was granted in 1923 in a letter to the Governor of the State of South Australia, Lieutenant-General Sir George Tom Molesworth Bridges.

SPAIN

Nowhere has the golf explosion been more pronounced than in Spain. There were only twenty-four clubs in existence here before 1965; the number had grown to fifty-one ten years later, and now, in 1988, the handbook of the Royal Spanish Golf Federation lists no fewer than ninety-eight, with about ninety courses.

Perhaps not surprisingly, the Spanish golf explosion has produced some very good golfers, or perhaps it has worked the other way round. Starting with their first golfers of world class, the Miguel brothers and Ramon Sota, Spain has produced as fine a crop of professional players as any country in the world in the last twenty years, led by Seve Ballesteros, who at his best is the finest golfer in the world. What a team this is: Ballesteros, Garrido, Piñero, Cañizares, Rivero and Olazabal.

Equally important has been the fact that Spain has produced some distinguished golf architects, notably the late great Javier Arana and now Jose Gancedo, so that the new courses are as attractive to the eye and testing to the player as any in the world.

Royal titles for golf clubs or other societies in Spain are largely divided between those

Right: *Don Juan, father of King Juan Carlos of Spain, who granted royal titles to the golf clubs of E1 Prat and Pedreña*

granted before the abdication of King Alfonso XIII in 1931 and those granted since the accession of his grandson King Juan Carlos in 1975. Of the eleven golf clubs in existence in 1931, half a dozen had the royal title, although rather surprisingly the oldest golf club in Spain at Las Palmas in the Canary Islands – located in the crater of a volcano – which was founded by British expatriates in 1891, only received the honour quite recently. The reason for this, I believe, is that in the early days the royal title was only bestowed if there was some actual connection between the Court and the club: if, for example, the King had played or visited the club.

Although there was no King of Spain between 1931 and 1975, the Franco regime proclaimed Spain a monarchy in 1948, but without a King. At that point Don Juan, Count of Barcelona, son of Alfonso XIII and father of Juan Carlos, who is today King of Spain, was the heir to the vacant throne. In this capacity he did not play any active part in the affairs of Spain, nor did he confer any honours except most interestingly the grant of royal titles to two golf clubs in 1956 – El Prat at Barcelona and Neguri near Bilbao – thus showing his great love for the game. At an earlier date, 1928, when Alfonso XIII was still on the throne, Don Juan played himself in at Pedreña, near Santander on the north coast, and granted the royal title there.

Today these matters are pursued much as they are in Great Britain. A club which wishes to gain the royal title states reasons why it should be so distinguished, and the merits of this proposal are evaluated by a National Sports Federation Committee. An application is then made to the head of the royal household, the Marques de Mondejar, who puts the request to the King, who then agrees or not to the petition.

Thanks to the kind help of the Secretario General de la Real Federacion Española de Golf, Don Luis Alvarez de las Asturias Bohorquez (a fellow-member, I was glad to find, of the R & A), it was possible to make an up-to-date list of the royal golf clubs of Spain. As in the UK, there are some distinctions to be drawn between those which are predominantly golf clubs and those, like our RAC at home, which are royal clubs for another purpose but own a golf course.

So I think we must make an arbitrary decision as to which clubs we think should be omitted, and it seems to me that the courses of the Royal Aereo Clubs of Santiago, Vigo and Zaragoza do not really bring them into the group we are trying to compile of golf clubs first and foremost. Reluctantly, too, I think the same applies to the Royal Automobile Club of Spain with its excellent Arana-designed course on the northern outskirts of Madrid. The Royal Equestrian Club which is listed among the golf clubs of Spain doesn't come into our classification as it doesn't own a course. Its excellent neighbour the Club de Campo Villa de Madrid is not royally honoured. A club near Madrid, Lomas Bosque, which assumed the royal title a few years ago, has been asked to desist.

After this exclusion process this is the list of the royal golf clubs of Spain:

1	Real Club de Golf Las Palmas (Canary Islands)	1891*
2	Real Club de la Puerta de Hierro (Madrid)	1904
3	Real Club de San Sebastian (north coast)	1910
4	Real Sociedad de Golf de Neguri (Bilbao)	1911
5	Real Golf de Zarauz (north coast)	1916
6	Real Golf de Pedreña (Santander)	1928
7	Real Club de Golf de Cerdaña (Puigcerda)	1929
8	Real Club Pineda de Sevilla (Seville)	1939*
9	Real Club de Golf 'El Prat' (Barcelona)	1954
10	Real Club de Golf de Menorca (Minorca)	1976
11	Real Golf Bendinat (Majorca)	1986

* Royal title granted in 1986.

The granting of the royal title of the Federation itself remains a mystery. Sr Alvarez de las Asturias Bohorquez told us the records had been lost during the civil war of 1936–9. All that remained were some old letterheads carrying the royal title, which at least showed that the honour was authentic.

This section ends with some personal reminiscences of a few of those Spanish clubs which I have enjoyed so much in days past. The following is based on my book *Famous Fairways* written in 1968:

> Javier Arana made his name with the big sweeping hilly course, the Club de Campo, on the outskirts of Madrid which is big in all senses of the word, indeed a little too big for me with its hills and dales. Subsequently Arana laid out a fine course near Bilbao on the north coast which I don't know, the Royal Neguri, and another, Guadalmina, on the Costa del Sol, which I do, in sight of the Rock of Gibraltar. I would suppose that Arana's best known and most famous course is 'El Prat', also a royal near Barcelona Airport, on land very close to the Mediterranean. This ground is virtually links-land, hard spare turf and sandy subsoil with liberal groves of umbrella pines and palm trees; a salt lagoon also helps to make life difficult. These pines make an exceedingly tight shot at the 140-metre third hole for example, while an unusual hazard, or rather interruption, at the short eleventh is an airport marker light. Although the ground is pretty flat some judicious building up and moulding of greens has been done and the flatness never becomes dullness. An excellent course.
>
> We return to Madrid for a short look at the oldest club there, and a royal one, the Real Club de Puerta de Hierro. Here is a course I have played often and once and once only in an Open Championship. I entered the Spanish Open in 1958 as a joke and nobody said me nay so I played though did not make 'the Cut'. Peter Alliss with whom I could possibly have been confused (by name not by play), in fact won, with a ridiculously low score; in his last round I saw him reach the eighteenth green from the tee, a distance of 385 metres, downhill, with his fifty-ninth stroke. It is true the Puerta de Hierro course then was very short with six par-three holes, four on the first half, including a formidable first hole across a deep cleft in front of the tee to catch an early morning top. These deep ravines, so deep as to be crossed by bridges, were a feature of the course. There were however plenty of two-shot holes, notably the old twelfth and thirteenth with the drive at each into a deep valley to be followed by a punch with an iron up to the green. Of the short holes, the third, to a small plateau green was the pick I think. Things are now changed with 36 holes, so that a longer and more demanding course is now provided.

The club was formed in 1904 and golf was first played at the race-course. It moved to its present site in 1911 on Crown land given by the King, who played his first game there in 1915. The course was terribly damaged in the civil war and a heroic effort was needed to get it going again.

In my playing days my favourite course in Spain was at Pedreña on the north coast, across the great harbour of Santander. This course produced that fine professional Ramon Sota and then the Ballesteros brothers. You used to embark in a small ferry called *Caddi II* and chug across the harbour to land at the club steps, and there you were. It was not great golf and there were no tremendous holes on it, but it was and is a most beautiful place to play golf at; on fine days the view up and down the coast is superb, the great bay and row behind row the whole chain of the Cantabric mountains, crowned by the snow-clad Picos de Europa to the westward. It was all good fun and your score ought to have been under 80 without bursting your boilers. The length was not and still is not great. There are some attractive trees on the course, otherwise it is heavily rolling hilly grassland with some delightful wild flowers, including the vivid blue Lithospermum, 'Heavenly Blue', in the rough at the top of the course by the 10th green. The course was designed by the British team of Colt, Allison and Morrison. Pedreña is strongly recommended and so at the end of the day is a visit to the Bar del Puerto in Santander for some fresh sardines grilled for supper, or other seafood, perhaps a lobster.

Coming now to the south, it was an unexpected pleasure to be greeted on Christmas morning at the Seville Club by a fine muster of peacocks; three proud males attended by a dozen hens and youngsters picked and pecked about the pine trees and shrubs in the warm winter sunshine at the door of the club house.

The Club here was founded in 1939 after the end of the civil war in Spain by the amalgamation of three original clubs in Seville, the Tablada Aero Club, the club attached to the racing club (Hipodrome) and the Pineda Club. The royal title had been conferred by King Alfonso XIII to the Tablada Club in 1923, and this title was transferred to the new joint club, which took the name of Pineda.

The Club is no great distance from the centre of the city, alongside the stables and stalls of the racing club, and its associations with the horse are borne out by the club badge which includes a horse's head supported by a golf-club and a polo-stick. The course is of 9 holes laid out among a variety of pines and can provide a test ranging from 5300 yards up to 6500 yards from the back tees. The course looked an attractive, well-shaded retreat from the hot summers of Andalucia. We were helpfully received here by the kindness of the Secretary, Don Luis Baron, and his uncle the General.

OUTSIDE EUROPE

The bestowing of royal titles upon golf clubs is not confined to the royal families of Europe. As we have seen in the previous chapter, the Sultans of Malaysia have been active and there are or have been royal titles in Swaziland and in Thailand.

My information on Bangkok is scanty, alas, although I was there on several visits. The *Royal Bangkok Golf Club* was formed as early as 1895 under royal patronage, and an early President was Prince Devawongsee. Its course is inside the race-course. The club house was an old Siamese temple. There seems to be a *Royal Dusit* in Thailand as well. There is also the *Royal Hua Hin* Club on the Gulf of Thailand, about 100 miles from Bangkok, dating from 1922 and well spoken of.

In the harsh deserts of the Middle East man was not deterred and has devised golf of a sort: sand fairways, browns instead of greens amid rock, scrub, scorpions and snakes, under a cruel climate in the inhospitable territories of the oil lands of the Middle East, largely it is true for the benefit of the expatriate workers there rather than the local inhabitants.

Royal Baghdad Golf Club

That invaluable work the *Shell International Encyclopedia of Golf* tells us that a 13-hole sand course was laid out near the city of Baghdad in 1925 when the Club was founded by British residents. The royal title, it seems, must have come from King Faisal or his son, the old Harrovian King Ghazi, or his grandson King Faisal II, who was deposed and murdered in 1958. Golf did not survive the new regime, and Royal Baghdad must now be numbered among the has-beens.

Imperial Country Club Teheran

In Iran there was a primitive rock-and-sand course at Tehran, so Shell tells us, in time past, and this was replaced in 1970 by an up-to-date grass course in modern style. I remember paying it a visit in 1973, out by the Hilton Hotel on the north side of the city, and a fine view of the Elburz Mountains

The club house of Royal Bangkok was described in 1901 as 'one of the quaintest installations of the Royal and Ancient game'

made a great backdrop. The course was designed up to full length by a British professional, Jack Armitage, once an assistant to Archie Compston at Coombe Hill. Another Armstrong course was laid out at Persepolis as part of the celebrations devised by the Shah to celebrate the 2500th anniversary of the founding of the Persian empire by Cyrus the Great. Any such manifestations of royalty were swept away with detestation by the downfall of the Shah and the dictatorship of the Ayatollah Khomeini in 1979.

Royal Swaziland

This is at Mbabane, in a small independent country alongside the Republic of South Africa and what is now Maputo, once the Portuguese Colony of Mozambique. The Club received its royal title from King Sobhuza II in 1966.

Dr Matsebula, the historian of Swaziland, reports that the King visited the Club for the occasion in Mahiya dress, the official tribal dress for the occasion, arriving at the hotel with his regiment, chiefs, wives and daughter, Princess Dlalasile.

The monarch teed off to symbolize the granting of the honour, while the royal wives sat on the Persian carpet for the ceremony in the hotel foyer. It was not confirmed how many of the King's wives attended; one report said that they numbered a hundred in total.

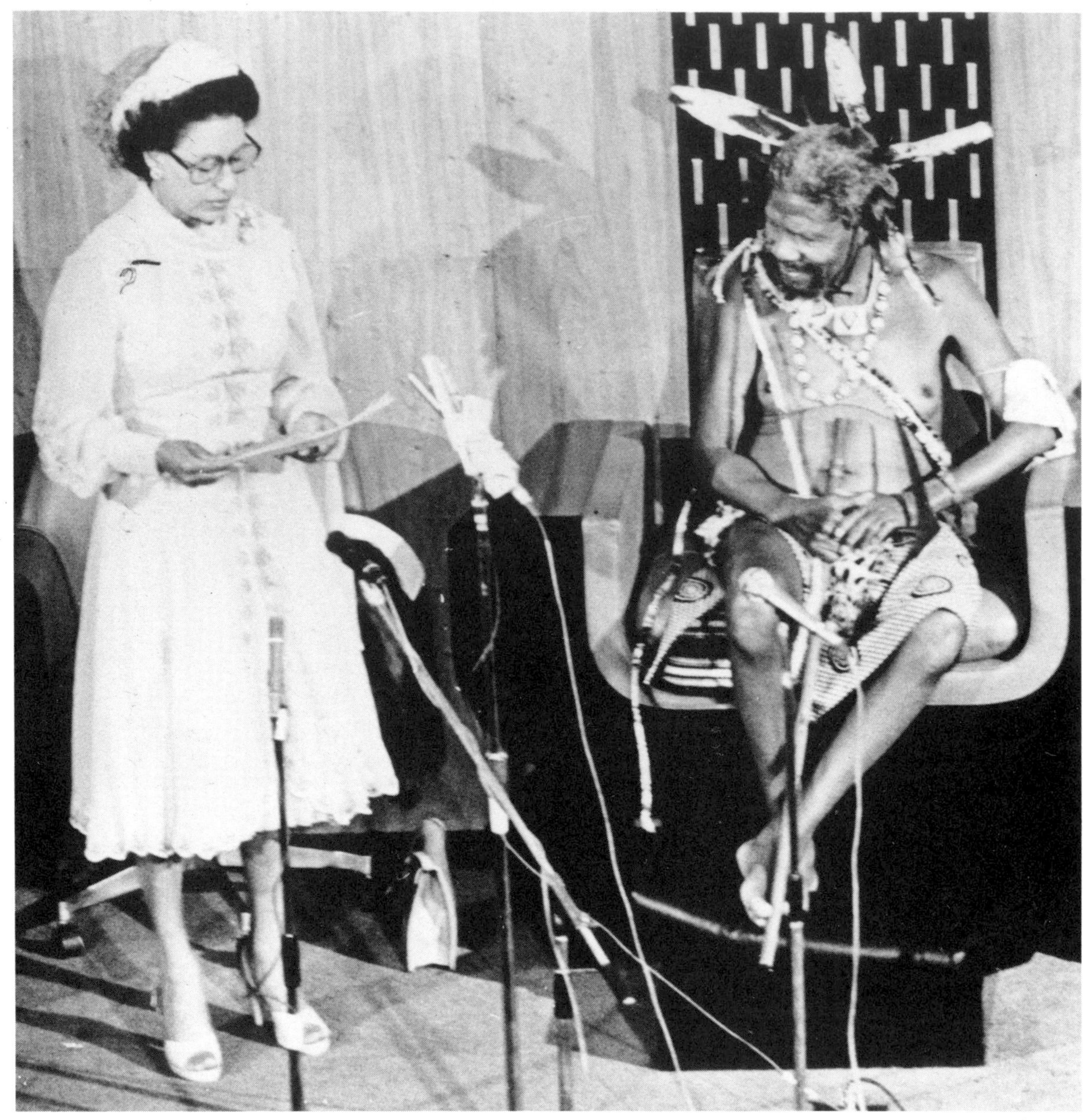

King Sobhuza of Swaziland at his Jubilee celebrations with Princess Margaret in 1982. He granted the royal title to the Swaziland Golf Club

Morocco

The latest royal adherent to the game is King Hassan II of Morocco, who today seems to be the only member of any royal family with an active interest in golf. I am indebted to my friend Alan Booth, who has visited Morocco a number of times, for the following description of the six royal clubs of Morocco:

> Golf is very much a Royal sport in Morocco. The country's emergence in recent years as a golfing centre, attracting visitors from all over

The magnificent Royal Dar-es-Salam in Rabat, Morocco – the venue of the Hassan II Trophy. Pictured is Irish professional Eamonn Darcy putting on the 8th green

the world, is the result of the support and patronage of Morocco's King, Hassan II, himself an enthusiastic player.

In his palaces at the ancient cities of Fez and Meknes, he has created nine-hole courses, and the country's finest course, Royal Dar Es Salam at Rabat, the country's capital, stands comparison with any around the world, not only in its spectacular surroundings, but in the quality of its golf.

Royal Dar Es Salam is one of Morocco's newer courses, being opened in 1971. Carved out of a 1,000 acre cork oak forest, its wide, lush fairways may appear easy, but call for accurate play, with many dog legs, strategic bunkers and artificial lakes to contend with, and many of the fairways completely lined by trees.

The championship Red course, with tees up to 100 yards in length, is stretched to almost 7,500 yards for professional tournaments, with a par of 73. It opens with a par 4 of 410 yards, not too difficult, but with a slight dog leg on the left, there are bunkers on either side, to catch a wayward shot. The second hole of 239 yards is the longest par 3 on the course, with a raised green surrounded by bunkers.

As with most of his courses, Trent Jones has created spectacular, contoured greens, the 3rd hole, a par 4 of 454 yards, having a long, narrow green giving little margin for error.

The 5th is the first of five par 5 holes, the

longest being the 8th of 575 yards, notable only for the approach to the green, the fairway running down into a hollow and climbing to a well bunkered green.

The short 9th of 199 yards brings water into play for the first time and takes its place among golf's most spectacular holes. The tee shot has to carry to an island green, reached by a rustic bridge, spanning a lake with flamingos and wild fowl, and with flowers and shrubs all around provides a glorious setting.

Water again comes into play at the 464 yards 11th, running along the fairway and green; at the 569 yards 12th, where the drive needs careful positioning over the lake, which edges all the way along the fairway to the green, and at the 225 yards 17th, where a pulled tee shot will finish in the water.

The 18th of 564 yards is a magnificent finishing hole, dog leg to the left, and only the longest hitters are able to reach a high, narrow green, in two.

Dar Es Salam's second course, the Blue, is another fine test of 6,825 yards, par 72, and there is also a nine-hole layout, the Green, of 2,387 yards.

In 1971, the King inaugurated an annual pro–am event, the Moroccan Grand Prix, the winner receiving the Hassan Trophy, a gem-encrusted ceremonial dagger. It is a tournament which has attracted the world's best players, among them Seve Ballesteros, Bernhard Langer, Sandy Lyle and Nick Faldo, and its winners have included former major champions in Orville Moody, Billy Casper, Johnny Miller and Lee Trevino. Peter Townsend claimed the only British win in 1978.

In 1987, Royal Dar Es Salam staged its first PGA European Tour event, the Moroccan Open, the first winner being Ryder Cup player Howard Clark, with an eight under par total of 284, to win by three strokes from Mark James.

Morocco's older courses include *Marrakech*, *Tangier* and *Casablanca*.

The Royal Club of Marrakech – the oasis city nestling at the foot of the snow-capped Atlas Mountains, and many times a haven for Winston Churchill, who found inspiration here for many of his famous paintings – is one of the favourite courses of King Hassan.

It was built in 1923 as a private course for the enjoyment of the then Pasha of Marrakech the Hadi Glaoui and later sold to King Hassan.

A short course of 5,255 yards, par 71, it winds its way through orange, cypress and eucalyptus trees, which provide the main hazards for the terrain is flat and not too demanding or strenuous. Even so, the fairways present a tight line from often elevated tees, and anything off line will find a resting place among the trees. The views are of course superb.

The Royal Club de Mohammedia, built in 1925, was Morocco's premier course until the opening of Dar Es Salam, and is an excellent test. Set between a river and the sea, along from Casablanca, of 6,634 yards, par 72, its opening holes are tree-lined, but then move among dunes to give it links characteristics along the Atlantic coast.

At Casablanca is located the *Royal Club d'Anfa*, set inside a race track and planted with flowers, a nine-hole course of 2,734 yards, par 67, opened in 1937.

Oldest of Morocco's courses is the *Royal Country Club of Tangier*, of 6,046 yards, par 72, opened in 1914. It was built by a British diplomat as a nine-hole course, surrounding a polo field, and was increased to 18 holes and redesigned by a British architect, the late Frank Pennink. An undulating course, it has plenty of variety and a fine setting, overlooking the bay of Tangier.

The Royal Club of Agadir, a nine-hole beautifully wooded course, has now been extended to 18 holes, with the King again commissioning Robert Trent Jones, who is also to develop other Royal courses with the increased popularity of golf for tourists to Morocco.

Right: *King Hassan II of Morocco*

The arrival of Brian Morgan's splendid new picture book *A World Portrait of Golf* brought two new royals to light: *Royal Nepal* at Kathmandu in the Himalayan slopes, the home of the Gurkhas, and *Royal Samoa* in the islands of the South Pacific.

An appeal to a friend in Kathmandu produced an excellent report on the Royal Nepal Golf Club, together with some photographs, from its Vice-President, Mr Robin Marston, as follows:

> What I imagine was a very rough and ready 18 holes was laid out in the late 1920s to the east of the city on an area that subsequently became the international airport. That built in the 1950s reduced the course to 9 holes. It was simply Nepal Golf Club up to that time.
>
> On 5th September 1965 it was bestowed with the 'Royal' title by H.R.H. Prince Basundhara Bir Bikram Shah, younger brother of the then King Mahendra. Both they, and the Crown Prince at the time (the present King) Prince Birendra Bir Bikram Shah played at the course on more than one occasion.
>
> In 1980 a further extension of the airport led, for the period of one year, to the total loss of the rest of the land which Royal Nepal Golf Club were occupying. Unfortunately it was Guthi land – the equivalent of Parish or Church land in the UK – we were given no compensation.
>
> However once the earthworks for the new airport terminal were completed in 1982–83 we were able once again to utilize spare land and have now developed a very interesting and challenging 9 holes using browns.

The Samoan course is on the island of Upolu, once a German colony and later administered by New Zealand. The Head of State is supposed to be elected for five years, but when independence was achieved one of the four Paramount Chiefs, His Highness Malietoa Tonumafili II, became ruler for life, and he no doubt is the nominal 'King' for whom Morgan tells us a special parking spot is marked out at the club house. The course, we learn, is of fair grassy quality.

Western Samoa is well known for Aggie Gray, who kept a hotel, well regarded over the years, and was brought to public notice in *South Pacific* and World War II. It is also famous as the last home of Robert Louis Stevenson, who is also recalled at Spyglass Hill in California. On his grave in Samoa is written:

> Under the wide and starry sky,
> Dig the grave and let me lie.
> Glad did I live and gladly die,
> And I laid me down with a will.
>
> This be the verse you grave for me:
> *Here he lies where he longed to be;*
> *Home is the sailor, home from sea,*
> *And the hunter home from the hill.*

SCOTTISH KINGS, QUEENS and PRINCES relevant to the story

James II	1430–60	
James III	1451–88	
James IV	1473–1513	Married sister of Henry VIII, whence claim to throne of England originated.
James V	1512–42	
Mary, Queen of Scots	1542–87	Executed by Queen Elizabeth.
James VI	1566–1625	Became James I of England in 1603.
Prince Henry	1594–1612	Elder son of James I; died young.
Charles I	1608–49	Second son of James I; beheaded.
	– Cromwellian gap of 11 years –	
Charles II	1630–85	Elder son of Charles I.
James II	1633–1701	Brother of Charles II; former Duke of York; deposed 1689.
Mary II	1661–94	Eldest daughter of James II; reigned jointly with her husband, Dutch William.
Anne	1665–1714	Second daughter of James II; last Stuart to reign.
James, the Old Pretender (James III)	1688–1766	Son of King James II; tried to recover the throne, 1715.
Charles Edward, the Young Pretender	1720–88	'Bonnie Prince Charlie'; son of the Old Pretender; tried to recover the throne for his father 1745. The last male representative of the Stuarts was Henry IX, second son of the Old Pretender, a Cardinal and a grateful pensioner of George III from 1799. He was reconciled to George III and left some crown jewels to the Prince Regent.

ENGLISH KINGS, QUEENS and PRINCES relevant to the story

King William IV	1766–1837	Third son of George III; succeeded his brother in 1830, married to Queen Adelaide of Saxe-Meiningen
Queen Victoria	1819–1901 (1819–61)	Niece of William IV; daughter of Edward Duke of Kent, fourth son of George III; married to Albert, Prince of Saxe-Coburg and Gotha, Prince Consort.
George, Duke of Cambridge	1819–1904	Son of the fifth son of George III; first cousin of Queen Victoria.
King Edward VII	1841–1910	Eldest son of Queen Victoria; Prince of Wales 1841–1901.
Prince Alfred, Duke of Edinburgh	1844–1900	Second son of Queen Victoria; sailor.
Prince Arthur, Duke of Connaught	1850–1942	Third son of Queen Victoria; soldier.
Prince Leopold, Duke of Albany	1853–84	Fourth son of Queen Victoria.
Prince Albert Victor, Duke of Clarence	1864–92	Elder son of Edward VII.
King George V	1865–1936	Second son of Edward VII; Duke of York 1892–1901, Prince of Wales 1901–10
Princess Louise, Princess Royal, Duchess of Fife	1867–1931	Eldest daughter of Edward VII.
Family of King George V	1894–1972 1895–1952 1900–74 1902–42	Edward Prince of Wales (Duke of Windsor), later King Edward VIII; abdicated 1936 and was succeeded by his brother Albert Duke of York, who became King George VI. Also younger sons Henry Duke of Gloucester, and George Duke of Kent.
Queen Elizabeth II	1926– 1921–	Elder daughter of George VI; married to Prince Philip, Duke of Edinburgh, son of Prince Andrew of Greece.

Index

Names of kings and queens are those of British monarchs unless otherwise stated.